PUB WALKS

The Cotswold Way

TWENTY CIRCULAR WALKS

Geoff Moss

COUNTRYSIDE BOOKS
NEWBURY, BERKSHIRE

First published 1996
© Geoff Moss 1996

COUNTRYSIDE BOOKS
3 Catherine Road
Newbury, Berkshire

ISBN 1 85306 408 4

To Rita and Tony for this life

Designed by Mon Mohan
Cover illustration by Colin Doggett
Photographs and maps by the author

Produced through MRM Associates Ltd., Reading
Printed by J.W. Arrowsmith., Bristol

Contents

Key for maps

[1]   Location of pub walk

•••.•••••••.•   Cotswold Way

→→→→   Pub Walk

→•••→•••   Pub Walk along the Cotswold Way

Publisher's Note

We hope that you obtain considerable enjoyment from this book; great care has been taken in its preparation. However, changes of landlord and actual closures are sadly not uncommon. Likewise, although at the time of publication all routes followed public rights of way or permitted paths, diversion orders can be made and permissions withdrawn.

We cannot of course be held responsible for such diversion orders and any inaccuracies in the text which result from these or any other changes to the routes nor any damage which might result from walkers trespassing on private property. We are anxious that all details covering the walks and the pubs are kept up to date and would therefore welcome information from readers which would be relevant to future editions.

Introduction

The Cotswold Way is a 104 mile long recreational path stretching from Chipping Campden in the north of Gloucestershire to Bath. The path follows existing rights of way along the Cotswold escarpment, providing glorious views, seemingly at almost every step of the route. It also passes through picturesque Cotswold villages, such as Broadway and Painswick, and the towns of Winchcombe, Cheltenham and Dursley, making it an excellent choice for the discerning walker who enjoys relaxing a while, away from the troubles of every day life.

The Cotswold Way, also referred to in this book as the Way, is usually tackled as a linear walk and as such provides an exhilarating experience. However, not everybody is able to devote the seven or more days required to complete this task. This book has been devised to provide the opportunity to sample the pleasures of the Way in manageable, pint-sized chunks, enabling the determined tourist and casual visitor alike the opportunity to make the most of their leisure time in this beautiful part of Britain.

Utilising pubs and inns on or near the Way, this book details 20 circular walks, starting and finishing at carefully selected hostelries, which enable the walker to enjoy, at least in part, the glories of the Cotswold Way. As each walk is completed, a fuller picture of the character of the Way is gained. The circuits have been organised to follow the Way from the northern starting point in Chipping Campden to the finishing point in the south, at Bath, by always following the waymarked route in a north to south direction. At the end of each chapter is a section dedicated to the long distance walker. Here, the Way is described from where it leaves the pub walk to where it joins the pub walk in the following chapter. The mileage in brackets represents the distance covered by this linking section. The aggregate mileage of that part of the Way covered in the walk and the linking section itself is shown at the very end of the chapter.

The pubs have been chosen not only for their location close to the Way but also for their suitability in providing a pleasant finale to an invigorating walk. Whilst everybody has their own idea of what makes a good pub, all these inns provide excellent food and drink in comfortable and clean surroundings. However, for maximum enjoyment of these facilities, the walker should take a few simple steps, before setting out, to enhance the overall walking experience.

Firstly, one should always telephone the pub before leaving home – a telephone number is provided in each chapter. Opening and meal times vary considerably according to locality and season and it can be disappointing to arrive at a country pub at the end of a walk only to find that no food is served on that evening. Secondly, whilst most pubs have parking facilities, these are normally for the use of patrons only and therefore it is common courtesy to seek permission from the landlord should you wish to use the car park while you walk. Where possible, alternative parking facilities close by have been suggested and if a car is to be left for several hours it may be preferable to use these rather than the pub car park.

Although all the pubs welcome walkers, it is recommended that a change of clothing and especially footwear is carried in the car, particularly in the winter months. Not only does it show consideration for the landlord but an otherwise splendid meal can be spoilt if one is wet and muddy.

Dogs can make wonderful walking companions but they must be kept under strict control, particularly where there is livestock. It is worth showing landowners and farmers that walkers are responsible people with respect for the property of others. The continued use of many of the paths often depends upon the goodwill of the landowners – and always remember that the enjoyment of those that follow is influenced by those who have gone before.

Each chapter contains a detailed guide to the individual walk and a sketch map of the route but it is recommended that the appropriate OS map be carried. The Pathfinder (1:25 000) is superb and ideal, though several would need to be bought, whilst the smaller scale Landranger (1:50 000), would suffice but does not always give the required detail. A map not only adds to the enjoyment of a walk by identifying landmarks and assisting the walker in making directional choices but also enables the walk to be lengthened or shortened as required. The appropriate sheet identification for both the Pathfinder and Landranger is provided in each chapter.

The approximate distance of each walk is noted but a time period for its completion is not. Suffice to say that a leisurely walking speed is 2 miles per hour and a fairly brisk pace will need to be set to achieve 3 miles per hour.

I am sure that you will enjoy many hours of walking using this book as a guide. Once you have completed all 20 walks you will have covered much of the Cotswold Way and enjoyed some of the best pubs and inns along its course. Perhaps it may inspire you to tackle the whole route, revisiting paths, villages and inns as if they were old friends. I hope that you will.

Geoff Moss
Spring 1996

Cotswold Way – Overall route from Chipping Compden to Bath (104 miles)

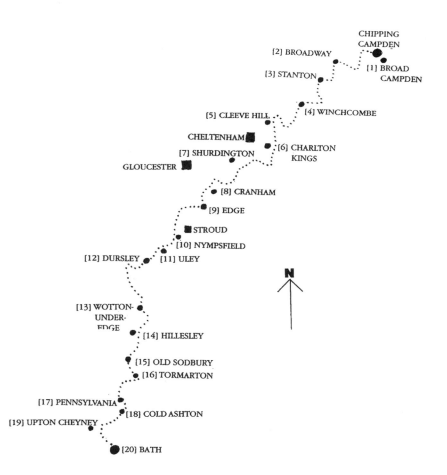

CHIPPING CAMPDEN

[2] BROADWAY

[1] BROAD CAMPDEN

[3] STANTON

[5] CLEEVE HILL

[4] WINCHCOMBE

CHELTENHAM

[6] CHARLTON KINGS

[7] SHURDINGTON

GLOUCESTER

[8] CRANHAM

[9] EDGE

STROUD

[10] NYMPSFIELD

[12] DURSLEY

[11] ULEY

[13] WOTTON-UNDER-EDGE

[14] HILLESLEY

[15] OLD SODBURY

[16] TORMARTON

[17] PENNSYLVANIA

[18] COLD ASHTON

[19] UPTON CHEYNEY

[20] BATH

N

Map showing the locations of Pub Walks 1–20

Cotswold Way – Chipping Campden to Stumps Cross (13 miles)

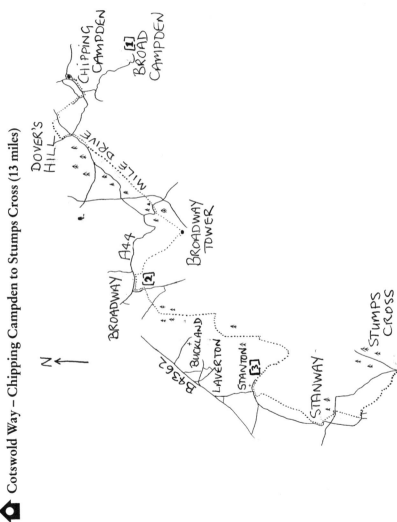

Map showing locations of Pub Walks 1–3

Cotswold Way – Stumps Cross to Dowdeswell Wood (16 miles)

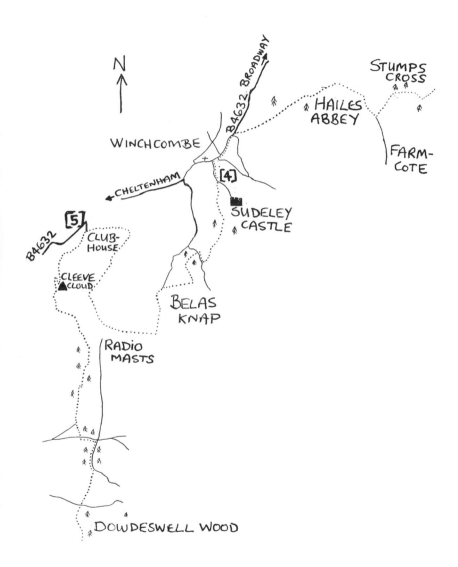

Map showing locations of Pub Walks 4–5

◆ Cotswold Way – Dowdeswell Wood to Painswick (19 miles)

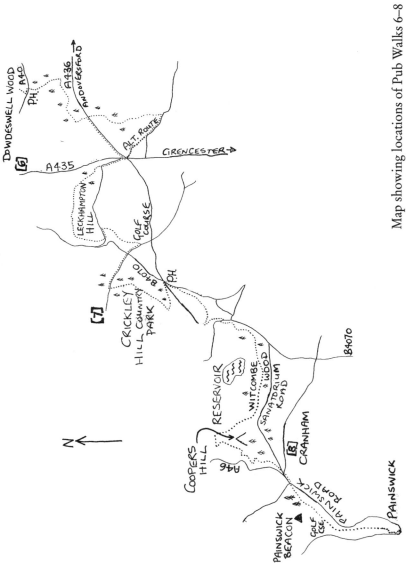

Map showing locations of Pub Walks 6–8

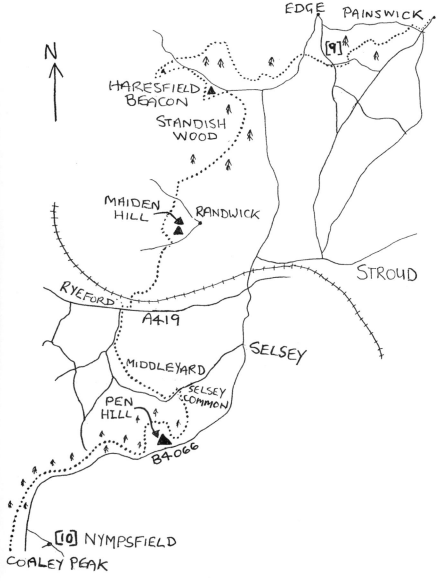

Cotswold Way – Painswick to Coaley Peak (14 miles)

N

EDGE   PAINSWICK

[9]

HARESFIELD BEACON

STANDISH WOOD

MAIDEN HILL

RANDWICK

STROUD

RYEFORD

A419

MIDDLEYARD

SELSEY

SELSEY COMMON

PEN HILL

B4066

[10] NYMPSFIELD

COALEY PEAK

Map showing locations of Pub Walks 9–10

Cotswold Way – Coaley Peak to Alderley (15 miles)

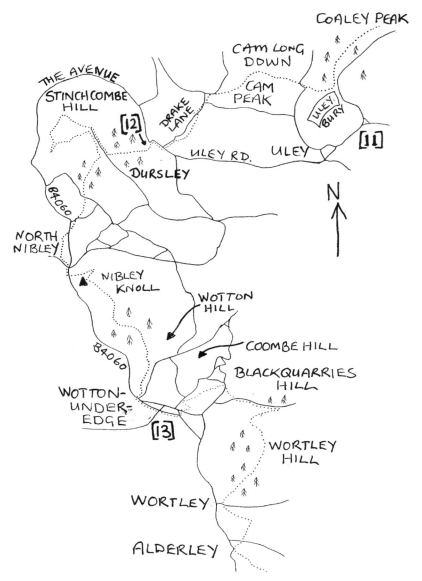

Map showing locations of Pub Walks 11–13

⌂ Cotswold Way – Alderley to Dyrham Park (14 miles)

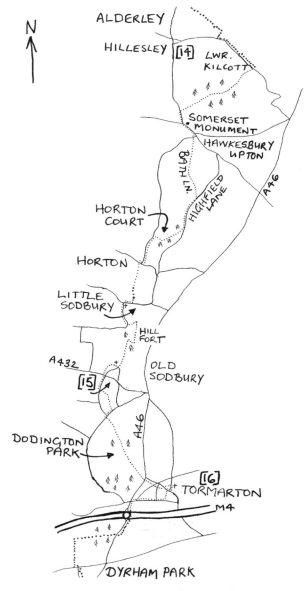

Map showing locations of Pub Walks 14–16

Cotswold Way – Dyrham Park to Bath Abbey (13 miles)

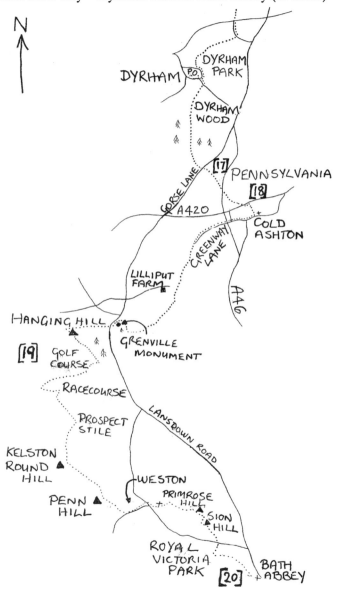

Map showing locations of Pub Walks 17–20

[1] Broad Campden
The Bakers Arms

Broad Campden is the little sister to Chipping Campden and lies about 1 mile to the south-east. As such it attracts a lot less attention than its larger neighbour but is no less attractive. It is not much more than a hamlet but is filled with picturesque cottages built of typical Cotswold stone and many of them are thatched. There is bed and breakfast accommodation available in the village.

Whilst a thatched pub with not one but two open log fires might set the pulses racing for the insurance company it has the opposite effect on the visitor. Situated at each end of a single stone-flagged bar area the hearths provide a warming environment even when not lit. One wall is adorned with a hand-woven rug depicting the pub and presented to it by a grateful customer, which is testament to the feelings enjoyed by those that make the effort to visit, which they do from all corners of the world. It is not unusual to hear conversations in a variety of accents about the discoveries of this marvellous area. Come prepared to join in and you will not regret that you did.

The pub offers a set menu supplemented by daily specials displayed on the blackboard above one of the fireplaces. The regular list contains a wide range of inexpensive favourites such as chicken Kiev, moussaka, chilli con carne, home-made pies of chicken or ham and leek, and mushroom or vegetable lasagne, to name but a few. Also available are assorted cheese ploughman's, a children's selection and various starters and sweets. The blackboard specials are no less impressive and include imaginative tempters such as cider and cheese chop, beef in bean casserole cooked in a real ale sauce and mushroom and nut fettuccine. If you have any room left for dessert spare a thought for toffee, apple and pecan nut crumble or morello cherry flan. The pub is a real ale enthusiast's delight, with no less than six well-kept beers. As it is a freehouse the selection is constantly changing but regularly featured are the local Stanway Stanney Bitter, Wadworth 6X, Eldridge Pope Hardy ale, Gale's HSB, Wickwar Bob and a guest beer. Draught Bulmers cider, Guinness and lagers are also on offer.

There is a garden with a children's play area for the summer months and the pub also offers accommodation. For those starting the long distance path the pub extends the walk by about 1 mile but with 100 plus to go and such a fine setting from which to start who cares anyway!

Telephone: 01386 840515.

How to get there: Leave Chipping Campden on the B4081 going south. Just out of the town centre turn off left on the minor road signposted to Blockley.

Parking: The pub has a good sized car park. Alternative parking can be a little tricky as the road is quite narrow and windy. However, with careful consideration to residents and through traffic it is possible to park the car safely.

Length of the walk: Approximately 5½ miles. OS maps: Pathfinder 1043 Broadway and Chipping Campden, Landranger 151 Stratford-upon-Avon (inn GR 158379).

A walk through a typically pretty Cotswold village and market town with a gradual climb to the escarpment edge. There are far reaching and glorious views of the Vale of Evesham.

The Walk

Starting with your back to the pub, turn left to round the corner and take the lane immediately to the left of the church. At the end of the lane, which opens out to a field opposite the last house on the left, head diagonally right to a point to the right of the second pole. This is marked by a footbridge over a stream, but do not cross it. Instead follow the right field boundary into the next field. Aim slightly to the right for a gap in the hedgerow, after which the path heads towards a clump of trees in the distance. Meet a stile before the trees, cross and steer to the right of the

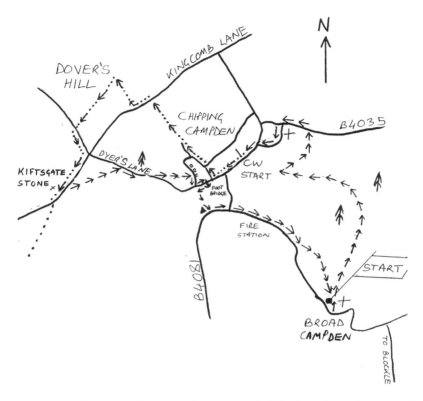

prominent oak trees, enjoying a clear view of Chipping Campden church.

Continue down the gentle slope, then pass through a field gate to a stile in the bottom corner. The indistinct path is diagonally across (a stone ruin acts as a good marker), turning right over the footbridge towards three wooden posts. Beyond these another footbridge is crossed, gaining the slope to a stone stile beneath the last tree on the right. Turn left onto the road and in 300 yards left again into Church Street, which is followed around to join the High Street.

The market hall in a short distance marks the official start of the Cotswold Way. Further along the street turn right opposite the Volunteer Inn into Back Ends, bearing left in a few yards up Hoo Lane, which becomes a footpath leading to a road at the top of the hill. Turn left and in a few yards enter a field on the right. Follow the field edge to a stile, which acts as a gateway to the National Trust land on Dover's Hill. The first glorious view from the escarpment soon appears as you walk to the left to read a panoramic dial. Exit the hill via the entrance to the car park, turning left along the lane. At the crossroads turn right and in 200 yards look for the Kiftsgate Stone, which was a meeting point for declarations in medieval times, in the wood on the right.

Leave the Way at this point by retracing your steps a few yards to take a footpath on the right across a field to a road. Turn right until meeting a thatched cottage, where a waymarked path opposite leads into a field. Cross diagonally right to the corner by some houses, passing between them to turn right through the estate. At the junction turn left and look for a path between the terraced houses in about 100 yards. Cross the footbridge beyond, immediately turning right. At the wooden pole turn left across the field, walk behind the houses and on emerging turn left. Turn left again by a black lamppost to the bend where the road to Broad Campden is taken.

Where the row of houses ends join the Heart of England Way on a path to the left behind the high hedge. Follow the path across the fields to a kissing-gate, then pass through and cross a private garden to a passage. On emerging, turn right along the lane to pass in front of a row of cottages. At the junction turn right to return to the Baker's Arms.

⌂ Cotswold Way — Kiftsgate Stone to Broadway Tower (2½ miles)

Continue along the road to where it bends to the right. Crossing a stile on the left, follow the path round to the right, which soon opens out into a wide, grassy, tree-lined avenue. This is The Mile Drive and where it narrows enter a field on the right, crossing it to a road. Continue on the same line in the next field to reach an information dial. Pass through the bushes to cross the busy A44 and continue through the trees. Once in the open aim up the slope to Broadway Tower to join Walk 2.

The length of the Cotswold Way covered by this chapter is 4 miles.

[2] Broadway
The Crown and Trumpet

The large village of Broadway with its Cotswold stone buildings straddles the busy A44 yet retains its charm. It continues to be a mecca to tourists coming to the area and at all times of the year the main thoroughfare is populated more with visitors than with local people.

The Crown and Trumpet lies just off the main road and so avoids many of the drawbacks of being in such a popular locality. In summer months its façade is adorned with a fine display of flowers, welcoming those prepared to venture away from the main street. Inside, this acclaimed pub still displays many of its 17th-century features yet caters for the modern day customer. There is a popular area to the front for sitting outside, which can be a delight on warm days, and on some evenings there is live music or a quiz night.

The menu is displayed on strategically positioned blackboards and draws its inspiration from locally produced ingredients such as prime beef from the neighbouring county of Herefordshire. Particular examples are the Evesham and Worcester home-made pies. The beer drinker is suitably spoilt for choice in this Wadworth tied house. On offer are Wadworth 6X, Morland Old Speckled Hen, Boddingtons Bitter, Flowers IPA and Original and Stanway Stanney Bitter. You will also find draught lager and stout together with a good range of low alcohol and soft drinks.

The pub offers good quality bed and breakfast accommodation and is situated directly on the Cotswold Way a little over 5 miles from the start.

Telephone: 01386 853202.

How to get there: Broadway is on the A44 between Evesham and Moreton-in-Marsh. Public transport is available by bus from either Cheltenham or Stratford. The Crown and Trumpet will be found down Church Street, which leads off the A44 by the village green, signposted to Snowshill.

Parking: There is a small area in front of the pub for patrons but it is probably better to use the public car park in the side road just a few yards further down Church Street.

Length of the walk: Approximately 3 miles. OS maps: Pathfinder 1043 Broadway and Chipping Campden, Landranger 150 Worcester and The Malverns (inn GR 095375).

A relatively short walk with a long, steady climb up the side of the escarpment towards Broadway Tower before returning on the Cotswold Way. There are excellent views.

The Walk

Walk away from the pub and main street to the church, turning left down a driveway and passing in front of some cottages. Go through two kissing-gates, turning right after the second to cross a stile and a footbridge over a stream. Turn left immediately to follow the hedgerow on the right to the top of the field.

Cross a stile and, in a few yards, another stile to enter a field on the right. The path lies up the middle of the slope but it is probably better to steer left around the rushes as it can get very wet. In the next field plot a course to the left of the tree stump, cross a stile and continue on the same line, heading for the far side of this field. A stile by a gate marks the beginning of a distinct path that navigates the side of the hill and finishes by another stile and gate at the head of a lane.

Walk up the lane to a gate, then bear left up the slope to the farmhouse. Follow the track to the right of the house then turn left before a wooden pole. The track is rough at first but soon becomes a metalled lane as the farm buildings are passed on the left.

The lane ascends and just before the crest you enter Broadway Tower Country Park by a stile on the left. It is necessary to remain on the public rights of way through the park or an admission ticket must be bought. Climb a large stile into the neighbouring enclosure, turn left to pass the

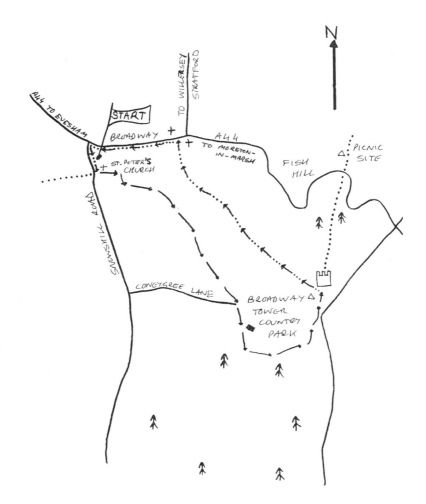

stone barn, now converted into a snack bar, then turn left through the large kissing-gate by the main entrance.

Walk to the back of the tower where the park is exited to join the Cotswold Way. Turn left to descend Broadway Hill, following the right boundary alongside several fields and using a distinct path. At a National Trust (Clump Farm) sign bear slightly right and at a waymarked wooden post take the path signalled diagonally right.

Traverse two smaller fields to a yard and lane which leads into Broadway High Street. Turn left to the village green, taking Church Street back to the pub.

Broadway.

Cotswold Way – Broadway to Buckland (1½ miles)

Starting at the Crown and Trumpet, walk for 200 yards away from Broadway. Just past the church turn right down a lane, pass through a kissing-gate beside a cattle grid and walk down the meadow to Waterloo footbridge. Continue across the next field to a lane and take the path immediately opposite. Follow the hedgerow on the right up the hill to Broadway Coppice. Pass through the wood and, on emerging, follow the left field edge to a wooden farm building by a lane which leads up from Buckland. There are no refreshment facilities in the village. Turn left onto the lane to join Walk 3.

The length of the Cotswold Way covered by this chapter is 3½ miles.

[3] Stanton
The Mount Inn

Stanton is a picture postcard Cotswold village with its honey-coloured stone houses, cricket pitch and pub. So much so that it receives quite a few visitors, who arrive to take photographs – but not the numbers that the likes of Broadway attract. Stanton quickly returns to peace and tranquillity, which is a joy to savour.

The Mount Inn is situated at the upper end of the village, out of sight. The road ends at the pub and there is quite a climb to reach it. Moreover, there are no signs either in the village or on the main road to give the secret away, so the establishment leads a peaceful existence and is largely the haunt of knowledgeable Gloucestershire folk. This gives it a laid back, unhurried atmosphere. Perched high as it is, it commands a magnificent view to be savoured throughout the year. However, simply the best time to come is at the end of a warm summer's day where the setting of the sun can be viewed from the terrace or garden. Inside, there is a spacious bar and dining area, and an open log fire to be enjoyed after a winter walk.

As the pub does not attract a large tourist trade the menu is not as extensive as some found elsewhere, but its quality is noteworthy. A daily specials board is displayed to supplement the selection of sandwiches, ploughman's and steak grills. The food is imaginative, illustrated, for

23

example, by the availability of a cheese fondue, though it will be necessary to persuade a companion to join in as a minimum of two persons is required for this option. The Mount Inn is one of only a dozen or so houses tied to the small independent brewery of Donnington near Stow-on-the-Wold, which supplies it with its two main ales – BB and SBA. Both are excellent and make up for the lack of choice, though draught lager is also available. The bar is well stocked with bottled beers and soft drinks.

The inn lies a few yards off the Cotswold Way, just under 10 miles from its starting point. Accommodation can be found in the village.

Telephone: 01386 73316.

How to get there: Stanton lies off the B4632 Broadway to Cheltenham road, about 3 miles south of Broadway.

Parking: The pub has a good sized car park and alternative roadside parking can usually be found in the village.

Length of the the walk: Approximately 5½ miles. OS maps: Pathfinder 1043 Broadway and Chipping Campden, Landranger 150 Worcester and The Malverns (inn GR 072343).

A stroll through three delightful villages before climbing up to the escarpment above Stanton. This is a particularly enjoyable walk on a summer's evening as the setting sun brings out the glow of the honey-coloured buildings. However in all seasons the view from the escarpment is spectacular.

The Walk

Walk downhill from the pub to turn right by the cross, along a narrow lane that leads to the church. Enter the churchyard, passing to the right of the building, and exit via a passage between two high stone walls. At the end do not go into the field but turn left to follow the tall hedge.

Enter the field by an iron kissing-gate, then bear to the left for 100 yards to cross a stile into the adjacent field. Keeping straight ahead, go over this field and four others to eventually cross a stile beside a house, into a lane. Turn right along the lane through the peaceful village of Laverton.

Follow the lane when it bends left, pass the village hall on the right and at the junction take the bridleway opposite. As the path emerges at the bottom of the gardens, climb the stile on the right, aiming to pass the wooden pole in the middle of the field.

Cross two stiles a few yards apart, catching a glimpse of Buckland church in the distance. The track follows the left field edge, and after a dip in the ground you cross a stile on the left. Follow the fenced-in path past the greenhouses and wooden buildings, after which the route crosses to

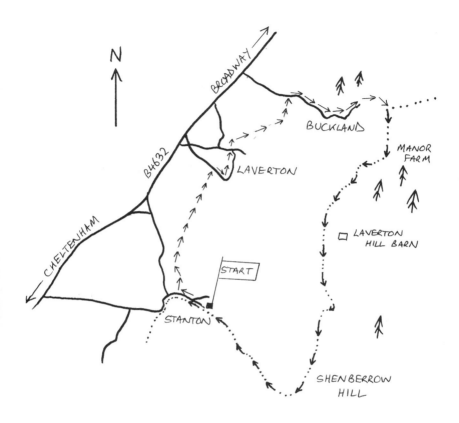

the other side of the fence. Pass through the squeezer stile. Turn right to follow the road as it bends and climbs through Buckland for ½ mile, ignoring the path ahead at the first bend. Pass the holiday cottages, the small lake and Burhill Farm, gently climbing the hill.

⌂ Just after a wooden barn on the left join the Cotswold Way. The lane soon becomes a rough track that leads to a gate at the entrance to a farmyard ahead. Turn right through the yard to follow the fence on the right through several gates and fields. The Way is still climbing and it goes across the hill, with good views to the right. In about a mile turn right to cross a cattle grid and follow the track to a gate to the right of a house.

Pass through the gate, cross the driveway leading to the house and descend right down the gulley, which is very slippery when wet, bearing to the left of a wooden-fenced sheep wash. Go over a stile into the next field, steering right to cross a brook. Over another stile the path continues to descend past some horse jumps to a pond. Turn right to cross two stiles in quick succession.

On emerging from the trees, turn left by a shed onto a wide track, which leads to Stanton. Leave the Cotswold Way in Stanton at the small grass area in front of a row of cottages by turning right to gain the hill back to the pub.

Cotswold Way – Stanton to Farmcote (4½ miles)

The Way continues downhill through the village of Stanton to a junction. Turn left to where the road bends right, continuing along the private drive to Chestnut Farm. In 100 yards cross a stile on the right into a field and continue ahead for six fields and the corner of a seventh to a lane. This is about 1 mile and the unusual thatched cricket pavilion on staddlestones can be seen opposite.

Turn left along the lane into Stanway, passing Stanway House, once the home of James Barrie – author of *Peter Pan*. Just after the public entrance turn left, passing in front of a cottage and through a kissing-gate onto a path leading to a road. Turn left for 50 yards, crossing the road with care to a path between two hedges.

At the end of the path cross three fields, with the hedge on your right, to a house. Pass through two gates to a lane, turning left to enter Wood Stanway. Continue through the hamlet to Glebe Farm after which the path becomes a rough track. Enter the adjacent field just before the wooden pole, bearing right up the slope to the left of the second pole. In the next field aim for a field gate below a house. Turn right up the bank past an oak tree to cross a stile. Go left to a large stile and in a short while bear right up the slope to a line of beech trees. Follow the stone wall to the road junction at Stumps Cross.

Immediately, turn a sharp right onto a wide track beyond a gate. This leads past some farm buildings to turn right just before a small copse. Follow the right field boundary around Beckbury Iron Age hill fort and at Cromwell's Monument descend across two fields to Salter's Lane, which leads from Farmcote to join Walk 4.

The length of the Cotswold Way covered by this chapter is 7 miles.

[4] Winchcombe
The Plaisterers Arms

Winchcombe, once an ancient capital of Mercia, is the quintessential Cotswold town and welcomes thousands of visitors each year without the tourism element being overbearing. Much of this is because many arrive at Winchcombe on foot as it is a haven for walkers. Four long distance/recreational paths pass through the town – Cotswold Way, Wychavon Way, Windrush Way and Wardens Way – and the attractions of Sudeley Castle and Belas Knap are within easy reach.

The Plaisterers Arms dates from the 18th century and has been a public house since 1830. It is so named because of the numerous previous landlords who also carried out the trade of plasterer. Fortunately, the current landlord and landlady dedicate themselves to hospitality, which they carry out admirably. The pub has an unusual split level design across two bars. A separate lower level Monks Retreat dining area can be found off the very comfortable and tastefully decorated Sudeley lounge. There is a garden and a patio area to the rear where children are welcome.

The menu offers a choice of hot platters including steaks, fish dishes, home-made pies, salads and vegetarian options. The standard list is supplemented by a daily specials board, with such treats as cauliflower and broccoli bake and chicken balti. There is a junior selection and also 'quick and tasty' meals for those wanting something less substantial. This is a freehouse serving Tetley Bitter, Wadworth 6X and Ansells Best Bitter, and the pub is also supplied by the recently formed Goffs brewery from Winchcombe itself. Draught Guinness, lager and cider are on offer too, while those eating may prefer to choose from the selection of wines.

Accommodation is available and the pub lies directly on the Cotswold Way, 17 miles from the start.

Telephone: 01242 602358.

How to get there: The inn will be found in the centre of Winchcombe, which itself lies 8 miles north-east of Cheltenham on the B4632.

Parking: There is plenty of public parking in the square in front of the pub.

Length of the walk: Approximately 7 miles. OS maps: Pathfinder 1067 Winchcombe and Stow-on-the-Wold, Landranger 163 Cheltenham and Cirencester (inn GR 024282).

A walk on some of the quieter paths around Winchcombe. There is a long, gradual climb up the escarpment, with splendid views, then you return to the town via Farmcote and Hailes Abbey. The Way, and our route, go directly past the abbey, which is owned by the National Trust and is open throughout the year. It was founded originally in 1246 and is mentioned in the works of Chaucer.

The Walk

Starting with your back to the pub, turn right and in a short way right again down the narrow Castle Street. After crossing a bridge turn left between two houses onto a footpath that leads to a kissing-gate. Bear diagonally right across the field to a lane. Turn left and in a few yards cross a stile on the right to enter a field.

Proceed towards some farm buildings, cross the yard to the field opposite and then bear up the slope along the same line to a lane. Cross the lane and stile, then continue up the hill for two fields. In the third field look for a waymarker directing the path between two bushes, turn left and then immediately right. Climb straight up the slope to a gate.

After pausing to enjoy the view that has unfolded behind turn left through the gate to follow the hedge to a waymarker, passing to the right of it into the bracken. Climb over the same fence, which has no stile, and start to climb the hill again. In a few yards look for a marker in the undergrowth pointing the way to the left at a fork. At the top of the slope turn left to pass through a small wood to a stile.

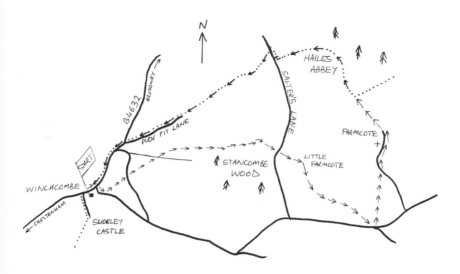

Descend to the right after a second stile and cross into the adjacent field on the right. Go over this and another field to a lane. Choose the rough track opposite to Foxcote Farm, passing through the yard, and on the other side turn right to walk across the top of the hill for two fields. Continue through a copse, turning right past a steel barn, beyond which the path meets a lane. Do not leave the field but turn back down the slope, which is signposted, to follow the right boundary of the next field. Arriving at a lane turn left to walk past the church and Hill View Cottage.

As the lane becomes a rough track and descends the Cotswold Way joins from the field on the right. Continue on the track, which becomes a metalled lane again, to Hailes Abbey. Immediately beyond, turn left into a field and aim diagonally across to the opposite corner. Bed and breakfast accommodation is available here at Pilgrim House (01242 603011). Pass in front of the cottages to a lane, then turn right for 200 yards before turning left onto a rough track.

In 400 yards turn right onto a field boundary and in a further 75 yards turn left to cross this and a further five fields, which includes the corner of one. The path eventually joins a lane, rough at first, which leads to a main road. Turn left onto the road, which takes you back to Winchcombe and the Plaisterers Arms.

Cotswold Way – Winchcombe to Cleeve Common (5 miles)

The Cotswold Way continues past the Plaisterers Arms, turning left into Vineyard Street. Cross the bridge and fork right before the

Vineyard Street, Winchcombe.

entrance to Sudeley Castle along a 'No Through Road'. In 400 yards turn right through a kissing-gate to aim diagonally across a field past a wooden pole. Continue on the same line for three fields to skirt around to the right of a fourth before crossing a field on the right.

Sweep around to the right, following the left boundary to a path that lies alongside an iron fence to a farmhouse. Continue past the farm buildings uphill on a rough track to a row of cottages, beyond which lies a road. Turn right along the road for ¼ mile, going left into a wood on a path signposted to Belas Knap. Emerge from the wood to follow the left boundary of two fields to the ancient long barrow.

Exit Belas Knap via a stone stile to walk the length of a field to a rough track. Turn left, walk for ½ mile and at the derelict farm buildings turn right to walk under the power lines. In a few hundred yards enter Cleeve Common via a gate to join Walk 5 by taking the path waymarked slightly to the right up the slope.

The length of the Cotswold Way covered by this chapter is 9½ miles.

[5] Cleeve Hill
The High Roost

As befitting its name, The High Roost is perched near to the highest point along the Cotswold Hills and overlooks the magnificent Vale of Evesham, with glorious views of the Malvern Hills in the distance. Once a hotel, the High Roost is a grand building not really looking like a public house at all. A flight of stone steps leads up to the imposing doorway and its two splendid bay windows provide an excellent vantage point from which to admire the panorama, though in fine weather the front terrace offers an even better setting.

There is an easy going feel in the pub itself as regular customers pursue their games of darts undisturbed by calling visitors. A small area is set aside for dining though food may be eaten at any of the tables. The menu is chalked on the blackboards above the bar and, whilst not offering an extensive choice, there is sufficient variety to be interesting. Regularly featured are rump and gammon steaks, barbecued trout and a vegetarian option. There is also a good selection of very reasonably priced desserts to finish off your meal.

The High Roost is a freehouse serving Hook Norton ales from its Oxfordshire brewery in the village of the same name. Hook Norton Best Bitter and the stronger Old Hooky are supplemented by Theakston XB.

Draught Guinness, cider and three lagers are also available.

The pub lies just a few hundred yards from the Cotswold Way at a point approximately 24 miles from the start. It does not offer accommodation but nearby bed and breakfast is available (eg: The Pines. Telephone Mrs Wilson 01242 674887). It is also just a short walk from the Youth Hostel on Cleeve Common.

Pub telephone: 01242 672010.

How to get there: The High Roost is midway between Cheltenham and Winchcombe on the B4632.

Parking: There is extensive parking at the pub and alternative parking to be found in a layby at the start of the lane leading to the municipal golf course off the B4632 at the top of the hill.

Length of the walk: 4½ miles. OS maps: Pathfinder 1066 Cheltenham, Landranger 163 Cheltenham and Cirencester (inn GR 989274).

The walk is almost entirely along the Cotswold Way as it does a tour of Cleeve Common. It is a largely easy going route, with only a couple of short climbs, and offers some good views of Cheltenham and the surrounding area. You are high up here, so take an extra layer on breezy days.

The Walk

Gain the hill from the pub along the grass verge, turning right along the lane signposted to the municipal golf course. At the clubhouse take the path ahead, which is sandwiched between two 'No Vehicle' signs, and then immediately fork right onto a track. In 75 yards notice the white post that has a black tip and the familiar Cotswold Way waymark. Look out for these posts as you make your way around the common.

In 400 yards bear right on the lower path to a waymarker directing the Cotswold Way up the slope, though those wishing to stay at the Youth Hostel should carry straight on at this point. A short climb brings you to Cleeve Cloud, which at 1,083 ft is the highest point of the Cotswold Hills, marked by a panoramic dial and an OS triangulation point.

After enjoying the view, turn right from the approach path to follow the markers across the hill before sweeping around the edge of the common to the prominent radio masts. Along this part there is an excellent view of Cheltenham and its racecourse, the original of which lies actually on the common. The walk departs from the Way in the dip immediately preceding the slope up to the masts.

Continue past the masts and another triangulation point, following a stone wall until it meets a wire fence. Turn left along the fence, which soon becomes a wall, as it descends to a gate on the right.

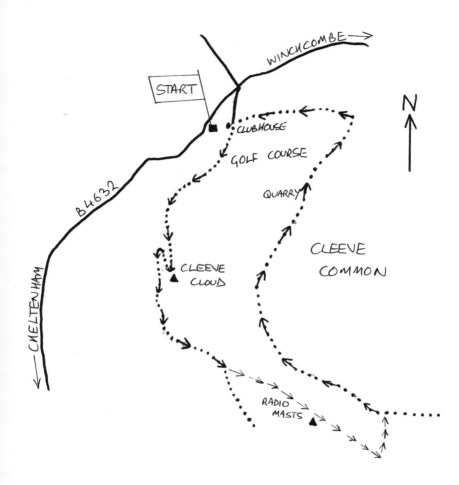

The Cotswold Way meets the common at this gate and the walk rejoins the Way by turning left up the bank. Carefully follow the marker posts for 2 miles as the route weaves its way across the common, descending through an old quarry, past the washpool, and then climbing sharply to emerge back on the golf course. Cross the fairway to return to the clubhouse and then retrace the lane back to the start.

Cotswold Way – Cleeve Common to Leckhampton Hill (9 miles)
Leave the common via a gate on the right in the dip immediately preceding the slope up to the radio masts. Select the bridleway between the two hedges and in a short way fork right. A further 100 yards on, turn right down the steep slope. The Cotswold Way then continues across the lower slopes of the hill whilst the masts can be seen up to the left. Be alert to the waymarkers regularly painted on any available surface, such as posts, trees and even stones.

Pass through the Bill Smyllie Nature Reserve and an old quarry to emerge at the head of a lane. Enter the adjacent field, then cross directly ahead on the field boundary to another lane. Turn left again to a crossroads and then go right to follow the lane to a point where it bends left. Climb a stile to a field.

Walk across two large fields and a lane and then continue into a third field. In 200 yards bear left down the slope to a stile between the farm buildings and a pylon. Cross the lane and turn right behind a hedge, which soon follows the edge of Dowdeswell Wood to a reservoir. Follow the concrete drive to the busy A40 and turn left. Refreshments are available here at the Reservoir Inn.

Beyond the pub the Cotswold Way leaves the road by turning right to enter a Woodland Trust area. Bear left up the slope for 300 yards then steer left into the wood. Climb a stile into a clearing and walk, with the wire fence on the left, to a field gate. Immediately after climbing the stile, turn sharply right to enter Lineover Wood. Pass through the wood to emerge in a field, with a farmhouse to the right. Climb the slope directly ahead to an old iron gate and 40 yards beyond it bear left steeply up the bank to the top of Wistley Hill. At the summit turn left through an iron field gate onto a wide farm track, which crosses a field to a road.

The original Cotswold Way turns right along the busy A436 but unless time is of the essence this is an unpleasant stretch. It is recommended that the alternative route, which is signposted, is taken by walking down the metalled lane opposite. After the entrance to the shooting range it becomes a rough track alongside the edge of a wood. Where it meets a pylon, aim across the field under the power lines to a white disc. Turn right onto a track which in a ¼ mile meets a lane.

Turn right along the lane, passing a farmhouse, and then when the lane bends left continue ahead on a track. This track is followed to the A435. Refreshments are available at the Hungry Horse inn opposite, but to continue the walk turn right and cross the road, going down the lane headed with a signpost, 'Gates'. When this lane bends left continue ahead on a footpath. Some 30 yards after a wooden walkway turn left and join Walk 6.

The length of the Cotwold Way covered by this chapter is 10 miles.

[6] Charlton Kings
The Little Owl

Once a village in its own right, Charlton Kings has long since been enveloped by the expanding spa town of Cheltenham. However, locals still refer to it as 'the village' and it retains much of that community spirit. Lewis Carroll is reputed to have written *Alice Through the Looking Glass* whilst a resident here.

The Little Owl, named after a winner of the Cheltenham Gold Cup, is not surprisingly decorated with racing pictures and memorabilia. Its plush and spacious interior is dedicated to providing a comfortable culinary experience, with the attached Annecy Suite dedicated solely to dining. The pub is very popular with local and Cheltenham residents so it is advisable to arrive early at any predictably busy times.

There is an extensive food menu, as one would expect, ranging from traditional ploughman's, salads and sandwiches to beefsteak and kidney pie in a Murphy's stout sauce. There is a range of grilled steaks, fish dishes and varying house specialities and a vegetarian option. If a full meal is not required a 'lite bite' menu is on offer. This is a Whitbread tied house serving Flowers Best and IPA, Wadworth 6X and Boddingtons beers. Murphy's stout and draught Heineken lager are also available. There is a wide selection of wines.

The Little Owl does not offer accommodation (try Mrs Mills at 35 Charlton Court. Tel: 01242 571690) and lies about 1 mile from the Cotswold Way at a point approximately 34 miles from the start.
Pub telephone: 01242 529404.

How to get there: The Little Owl lies on the Cheltenham to Cirencester road (A435), on the easterly outskirts of Cheltenham, 2 miles from the town centre.

Parking: A large car park adjoins the pub and alternative parking may be found in the nearby side roads.

Length of the walk: Approximately 7 miles. OS maps: Pathfinder 1089 Gloucester and Birdlip, Landranger 163 Cheltenham and Cirencester (inn GR 964199).

A long and fairly stiff climb up to the escarpment, is rewarded with a level yet exhilarating ramble across the hilltop, past the Devil's Chimney, before encircling Leckhampton Hill and descending again to the village.

The Walk
Walk away from the pub towards Cheltenham for 200 yards, then turn left into Bafford Approach. Take the second left into Longway Avenue and, where the road bends right, continue ahead on the footpath between the houses to the golf course, which is signposted to Sandy Lane.

The path lies diagonally right across the course but it is not clearly marked. Therefore, it is probably easier and safer to turn right to follow the inside edge of the boundary to the corner, then turning left along the far boundary. Look for an old iron kissing-gate in 300 yards that leads into Sandy Lane. If you do, however, decide to cross the golf course, take care.

Turn left in Sandy Lane and continue on a rough track which gradually climbs the hill face. When the track forks keep left on the lower path until it levels out, joining a wider track merging from the right. Turn left to walk with a steep grassy slope on the right for half a mile to a Y-shaped junction. Turn right to join the Cotswold Way.

Follow the path along the top field edge to and through a small coppice, after which the path continues straight ahead across Hartley and then Leckhampton Hills, with good views of Cheltenham. Keep fairly close to the edge of the escarpment, at the same time following the familiar Cotswold Way waymarkers. After passing a panoramic dial and triangulation point it is worth a short detour to drop down a few feet to view the Devil's Chimney, which is an oddly shaped stack of rocks steeped in local folklore.

The walk progresses across the hilltop edge to a lane just past an old

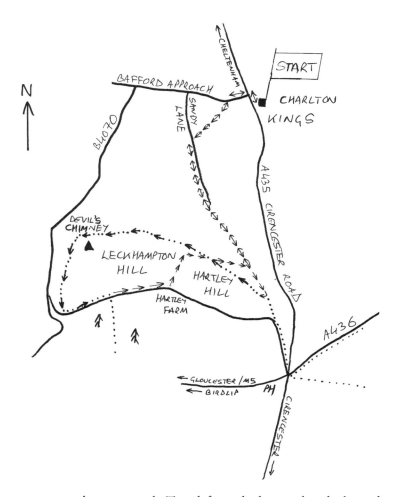

quarry now used as a car park. Turn left up the lane and at the brow leave the Way, which turns right at this point, and walk to Hartley Farm. In the farmyard turn left beside the metal barn onto a rough track signposted to Leckhampton.

Leave the track via a stile, pass a stone ruin and cross another stile. Follow the fence to a further stile that leads back onto the edge of the hill. Turn right and a few yards after a wooden seat take the path downhill until it reaches a double set of crosstracks. Ignore all paths leading off by entering into the trees ahead and turn left onto the path which brought you up the hill. Retrace your steps exactly back to the pub via Sandy Lane, the golf course and Bafford Approach.

The Devil's Chimney, Leckhampton Hill.

Cotswold Way – Leckhampton Hill to Crickley Hill

Leave Walk 6 at the brow of the lane just after the old quarry used as a car park by turning right onto a bridleway, which passes the Cotswold Hills golf course. Emerge opposite the National Star Centre for the disabled and turn right along the lane to a crossroads. Continue straight over onto a narrower lane and when it begins to descend into the trees join Walk 7 by climbing some steps on the left to a stile giving access to Crickley Hill.

The length of the Cotswold Way covered by this chapter is 3½ miles.

[7] Shurdington
The Bell Inn

Shurdington, just a few miles from Cheltenham, nestles at the foot of the escarpment with good views up to it.

The Bell is easily found, lying as it does on the main road bisecting the village, and was once a bakery. Fortunately for the hungry and thirsty walker, it now carries a very favourable reputation for good food and is always popular. There are two bars, with the lounge bar having a conservatory added to it to provide a very pleasant dining area. A lot of work is done here for local charities, with regular quiz nights and other fund raising activities plus live music nights. In the summer a spot of cricket watching can be enjoyed from the garden to the rear.

An extensive menu is supplemented by a daily specials board, which may include such treats as leek and ham pie in a Cumberland sauce, carrot and almond loaf and chilli braised mushrooms, all reasonably priced. Bar snacks are also available, such as salads, ploughman's, omelettes and sandwiches. A children's menu will keep the junior walkers satisfied. As for drinks, the Bell offers Gales HSB, Flowers Best, Original and West Country Pale Ale, the excellent London Pride from the Fuller's brewery of Chiswick, Wadworth 6X and Boddingtons. Draught Scrumpy Jack cider, which is very strong, two lagers and two stouts complete a first class choice.

The Bell, which does not offer accommodation (try the Original Yew Tree Farm. Tel: 01242 862022), lies over a mile from the Cotswold Way at a point approximately 37 miles from the start. Those walking the complete route may find the Air Balloon, which can be found on this section, more convenient, though anyone making the detour to Shurdington will not be disappointed.
Pub telephone: 01242 862245.

How to get there: The Bell Inn is about 4 miles from Cheltenham on the A46 Stroud road.

Parking: The Bell has its own car park but it can get very full at all times. There is a small public car park, separated from the pub's by a hedge.

Length of the walk: Approximately 7½ miles. OS maps: Pathfinder 1089 Gloucester and Birdlip, Landranger 163 Cheltenham and Cirencester (inn GR 923186).

A long, fairly tough climb up the escarpment but rewarded with good views on a clear day. The route continues through Crickley Hill Country Park before returning via Shurdington Hill.

The Walk
Cross the road from the car park to walk away from Cheltenham and, 100 yards beyond a bus stop, turn left through a kissing-gate into a field. Go straight ahead to the right corner, climb the short bank and continue on the path as it snakes through the hedgerows for 50 yards or so.

Look for a stile on the right, cross and turn left to climb more steeply. Halfway up the slope is another stile, after which the path bears slightly left, passing through a few trees onto distinctly higher ground. The path soon becomes more clear as it traverses the hillside, swinging left when it meets a line of wooden poles.

Turn left up the slope along the line of the poles to the crest beyond the last one. A glorious 180° panorama can be enjoyed from this vantage point. Leave this viewing area via the path leading away from the hill into a wood over a stile. Follow the path ahead at all times through the wood to a man-made clearing and gate.

Join the Cotswold Way by turning right to climb some steps to a stile that gives access to Crickley Hill Country Park. The path finds its way across the hill through woods, in roughly the same line, to the car park and visitors' centre. Continue beyond, again in the same direction, across the hill until the path meets a stone wall from the left. Double back to follow the wall to and through a wood to a road, which you cross carefully to continue on the pavement around the Air Balloon

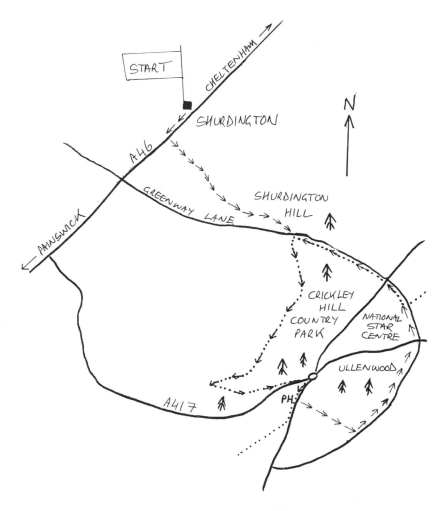

pub. At the entrance to the car park leave the Way by crossing the road to a footpath signposted to Cowley. Walk through the copse and, on emerging, turn left across a field towards a white disc marker.

Aim for a similar disc in the next field, at which you enter the adjacent field. Walk beside the right hedgerow to a gate. Turn left along the metalled lane alongside a stone wall. In 400 yards, where there is a signposted path indicated to the right, continue straight ahead, going gently downhill to a road junction.

Cross to the lane opposite, which leads past the entrances to the golf club and National Star Centre to a crossroads. Continue along the narrower lane ahead to where it starts to descend into the trees and bear right through the gate.

This is the path that was followed at the start of the walk and the route back is retraced carefully through the wood, down the slope by the wooden poles, turning right for a short way before continuing down the hillside back to the road and the pub.

Cotswold Way – Air Balloon pub to Cranham Wood (4 miles)

Shortly after the pub car park bear right along the concrete path away from the road. In 75 yards turn right into the trees and follow the path across the side of the hill, with excellent views to the right. Eventually, enter a wood via a stile and the path then dog-legs through the trees to arrive at a road.

It is, however, worth a short detour where the path dog-legs to enjoy the view from The Peak which is far reaching.

To continue, cross the road to the right and descend down a narrow path, turning left at the bottom onto a path that meanders through Witcombe Wood with sneak glimpses of the reservoir to the right through the trees. After ½ mile turn right onto a wider track and carefully follow the Cotswold Way markers to a gate. The Haven Tea Garden is just beyond to provide refreshments and it is here that Walk 8 is joined.

The length of the Cotswold Way covered by this chapter is 6 miles.

[8] Cranham
The Black Horse Inn

Cranham is just off the A46 between Cheltenham and Stroud and is often missed by the tourist. However, Gloucestershire folk know it to be a pretty Cotswold village in good walking country with an excellent, unspoilt pub.

The Black Horse is a fine stone building which nestles neatly in the centre of Cranham. Its stone-flagged floors, latched oak door at the main entrance and welcoming open fire in the winter months make it a perfect example of a country pub and its ambience is created by chattering voices and chinking glasses, unspoilt by background music.

It is advisable to arrive early or be prepared to sit and soak up the atmosphere as the establishment's reputation for good food makes it a popular choice for many, particularly at weekends. Choosing from the ever changing and imaginative 'blackboard' menu can prove to be enjoyably problematic in itself. For example, would you select Homity Pie, a cheese and potato local speciality, or baked trout with almonds? Perhaps you would prefer cauliflower cheese with Cumberland sausage or avocado with prawns? There is also traditional pub fare such as cottage pie, gammon steak or chicken tandoori. A roast is offered at Sunday lunchtimes. Whatever is chosen, be prepared to have a healthy appetite as the portions served are very generous. The drinker is also well catered for, this being a freehouse with a good range of real ales on offer. Beers generally available are Hook Norton, Marston's Pedigree, Flowers Original and IPA and Boddingtons Bitter. There is Murphy's stout and Stella Artois lager on draught plus a wide choice of bottled beers, soft and low/non alcoholic drinks.

The Black Horse does not offer accommodation (try Castle Lodge on 01452 813603). It lies less than 1 mile off the Cotswold Way at a point 45 miles from the start.

Pub telephone: 01242 812217.

How to get there: Cranham is situated east of the A46 between Cheltenham and Stroud, some 9 miles from Cheltenham. The signposted turning to the village is just under 1 mile south of the entrance to Prinknash Abbey.

Parking: The pub owns a sizable but rough car park to the right of the building. However, there is a public layby on the left by the 'Cranham' village sign. It is then only a short walk along the road to the centre of Cranham and the pub.

Length of the walk: 4½ miles, with a shorter option of 3 miles. OS maps: Pathfinder 1089 Gloucester and Birdlip, Landranger 163 Cheltenham and Cirencester (inn GR 897130).

A fairly easy stroll on generally level ground, with only two short, steep ascents, one rewarded by a good view from Cooper's Hill. Mainly through woodland, including the Buckholt Nature Reserve – as this is purely a woodland reserve, dogs are allowed the freedom to run around.

The Walk

Starting with your back to the pub, turn right to the junction and then right again. At the crossroads by the village hall turn left onto a wide track and in 150 yards fork left to follow the track straight ahead, ignoring all other paths leading off, then cross a stream via a footbridge. As the path climbs out of the valley it becomes a metalled lane.

At the junction with a road, turn left for 50 yards before steering right onto a track that descends straight ahead. After a Buckholt Wood sign fork right to gain a view of the reservoir between the trees. In 75 yards join the Cotswold Way by turning left.

Follow the main track at all times, keeping a keen eye for the numerous familiar Cotswold Way waymarkers as the route winds itself around the side of the hill. After you pass through a gate onto a metalled lane refreshments can be taken at the Haven Tea Garden.

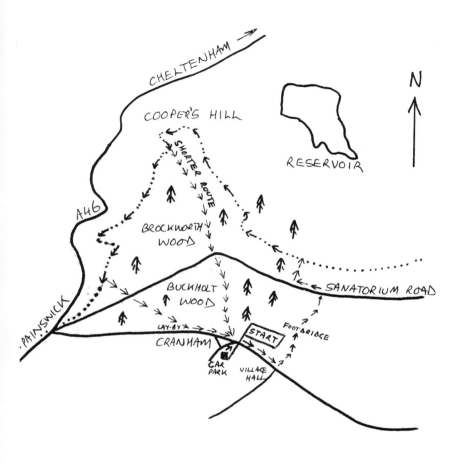

Continue along the lane to a small cluster of houses with a red letter box and bear left of Stonely Cottage. Take some time to look up the slope of Cooper's Hill on the left and imagine chasing a Gloucester cheese down it, as the locals do for fun (!) each Whitsun Bank Holiday.

Pass through a kissing-gate to take the first left and then left again to climb to the top of Cooper's Hill with its view. Notice the cockerel perched on the pole marking the summit and remember to peer over the edge to where you were just a few moments before.

To take the shorter route back, walk away from the hill, selecting the track on the left of three up the bank. Follow this path for 200 yards to a footbridge and turn left. In a few yards, after the low wooden barrier, fork right to follow the wide track to a building. Pass through the gate to a road, turn left and then right onto a footpath that enters the wood. Descend the path, keeping straight ahead to a forking of tracks. Bear right then almost immediately left, continuing to descend. At a small clearing where several tracks meet choose the small path opposite. Descend for a few yards and take the path on the right to cross a stream. Ascend the bank to emerge opposite the lane leading to the pub.

To take the longer route back, walk away from the hill, selecting the track on the right of three and still following the Cotswold Way waymarkers. As the path descends and bends right, turn left onto a lower track and proceed to a squeezer stile. Turn left and descend, then fork right and continue along the track as it widens and meanders through the wood. Keep looking for the waymarkers on the trees.

At a crosstracks, bear left up a steep ascent, which soon runs parallel to a stone wall. At a Buckholt Wood Nature Reserve sign leave the Way at the tree in the middle of the path by forking left to descend, following the yellow and orange arrows. Cross the road to take the track to the left of another Buckholt Wood sign, forking right shortly to gently descend. Keep straight ahead until a small car park, which is the alternative parking option, is reached. Turn left onto the road which leads into the village and the pub can be seen off to the right.

Cotswold Way – Cranham Wood to Edge (5 miles)

Shortly after a short but steep ascent the path meets a tree. Walk 8 continues to the left but the Cotswold Way continues right, gently descending through the wood to a road. Turn right, crossing the main road, and immediately enter Pope's Wood. In 150 yards bear left and in a further 75 yards cross a lane to enter Buckholt Wood Nature Reserve.

Take the path that lies directly ahead, following it until it joins a lane. Continue to a house, after which bear right onto a footpath leading onto Painswick golf course. If time permits it is worth, on a clear day, detouring to enjoy the view from Painswick Beacon. To do this, continue along the rough track beside the wall, steering left to the OS column marking the summit. Carry on down the old quarry edge to rejoin the Cotswold Way at a meeting with a lane.

The Way itself aims unerringly through the middle of the fairways of the golf course, passing a coppice on the left until it meets a lane. Turn left and then right onto a rough track. This soon becomes a gravel path and diverts left onto a narrow path through a wood. Emerge uphill from the clubhouse and cross the fairway with care to the corner of a stone wall embracing the cemetery. Walk to the right of the wall, descend the gentle slope and enter the copse by some houses. Turn right along Golf Course Road to a junction and turn left into Painswick.

Look for a telephone box and steer right into a 'No Entry' road. At the end turn right into New Street, passing the church, after which the Cotswold Way enters Edge Road. Bed and breakfast accommodation is available at Hambutts Mynd (01452 812352). Where a high stone wall finishes turn left into Hambutts Field, descending to the bottom corner, and cross a stile to follow a narrow path through the houses.

Cross another stile to descend the right field boundary to aim for a white disc in the next field, beyond which a further stile is crossed. Continue downwards to an old mill, which is now a private residence. Bed and breakfast can also be found along the lane at Upper Doreys Mill (01242 812459).

The Way passes behind the house to a metal barn. Take the track right up the slope and in 75 yards cross a stile into a field. Turn right to a wood, cross a footbridge and, on emerging, turn left to walk steadily uphill across two fields to a lane. Turn right to a junction, joining Walk 9 at the car park of the Edgemoor Inn.

The length of the Cotswold Way covered by this chapter is 6 miles.

[9]   Edge
The Edgemoor Inn

Edge is a small village just a few miles from its very picturesque and more well-known neighbour Painswick. Its elevated position means that it looks down the valley to Painswick and there are several very pleasant spots to sit and enjoy this delightful part of the Cotswolds.

The Edgemoor Inn is constructed of typical Cotswold limestone, giving it a familiar honey-coloured façade. Inside, much time and money has been spent to modernise the furnishings without detracting too much from the village feel. The interior is divided into two areas – a section for eating and drinking and a larger one set aside for dining, where smoking is not permitted. There is also a terrace that, on a clear day, gives a magnificent view of Painswick.

As one would expect from a pub that derives much of its trade from food-related custom there is an extensive choice of meals and snacks. A set menu lists basket meals, sandwiches and jacket potatoes and is supplemented by a specials board. This offers home-made pies, curries and vegetarian dishes plus some very tempting desserts. Come prepared to ponder long and hard before making your final selection, and enjoy a meal in very comfortable surroundings. This is a freehouse serving Hook Norton Bitter, the fruity Smiles Best Bitter from Bristol, Uley Old Spot from a small independent brewery a few miles along the Cotswold Way, Tetley Bitter and a new-style smooth keg beer called Kilkenny. There are also two draught lagers.

The Edgemoor Inn lies directly on the Cotswold Way at just over 49 miles from the start and overnight accommodation can be easily found in Painswick.

Telephone: 01452 813576.

How to get there: Edge lies just west of Painswick but is more easily approached from either Stroud or Gloucester. Situated on the A4173, it is 5 miles from Gloucester and 4 miles from Stroud.

Parking: There is a large car park adjoining the pub and a little off road alternative parking opposite.

Length of the walk: Approximately 6 miles. OS maps: Pathfinder 1113 Stroud, Landranger 162 Gloucester and Forest of Dean (inn GR 850091).

A fairly level walk, mainly through woodland, with an excellent viewing point from Haresfield Beacon.

The Walk

⌂ Cross the road at the far end of the car park to take the path signposted to Haresfield Beacon. In 75 yards turn right and in a further 100 yards bear left up the bank to follow the Cotswold Way

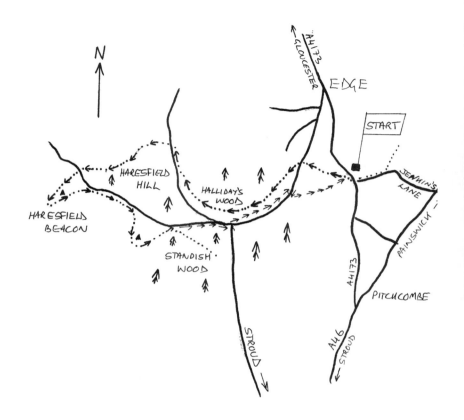

markers across the old quarry to a road. Continue on the signposted path, passing through a wood before turning left onto a rough track.

Pass the hexagonal-shaped house called The Reddings, onto a bridleway, which leads through the wood to a lane. Turn right, walking for ¼ mile to turn left past an old well. Walk for a further mile, passing the Cromwell Monument Stone, to Ringhill Farm. Turn left and then in 30 yards turn right up the slope alongside a barn. Take the path to the right of a field to a stile, which gives access to Haresfield Beacon and an excellent view of the Severn Vale.

After enjoying the view, walk away from the beacon on the opposite edge of the hill to the approach path. Leave the hilltop via a stile to travel through a small wood and at a junction with a lane turn right down some steps. Follow the path to cross a stile into an open field. Bear right to the triangulation pillar, at which the route crosses to the left of a cluster of trees to a National Trust car park.

Here leave the Cotswold Way, which continues on the path into Standish Wood, and go right along the road. Where this ends at a junction turn left into Stockend Wood, immediately turning right onto a path, which bends in a 'S' shape where it crosses another coming from the road. Continue to walk on a parallel course to the road until the path bends to the right to join the road via a stile.

Turn right for 50 yards to a path signposted to the left to Painswick. In a short way fork to the right to follow a small wall. The path widens into a track and there is a good view of Painswick church in the distance. Keep on a narrow path close to the hedge but as it begins to descend change line slightly to the left, aiming directly for the church spire. Enter the trees and at the cross-tracks keep straight on to emerge opposite the pub car park.

Cotswold Way – Standish Wood to Coaley Peak (9 miles)

Leave Walk 9 at Cripplegate car park by entering Standish Wood. Immediately take the left path and in ½ mile fork right where three paths meet. The wood can be delightful, particularly in late spring, and the walking is easy. Overnight camping can be had at a designated National Trust location here but there are no facilities other than an open space!

Carefully follow the Cotswold Way markers through the wood, eventually turning right onto a concrete but mud-covered bridleway. Emerge atop Maiden Hill with good views to either side and walk beside the drystone wall ahead. In the second field turn left then immediately right to cross two fields to a passage between houses.

Turn right in front of the houses for 150 yards before going left into a field. Aim down the slope to the right, continue ahead across two more fields and then turn right at a beech tree. Walk with a hedge on your left to the next field, cross to a stile and then walk through two smaller fields. As a third field is entered bear left down the slope to cross the railway line via a footbridge.

Walk by the side of the playing field to the Stonehouse to Stroud road. Bed and breakfast accommodation is available at Merton Lodge, which is just a few yards to the left. The Way continues to the right to a mini roundabout, where it turns left to descend over the Stroudwater Canal via a humpback bridge and enters Ryeford.

Cross the main road using the pedestrian crossing and continue ahead along Ryeford Road (South) into King's Stanley. Pass Stanley Mill and just after a small bridge over the river Frome turn left over a stile into a field. Walk with King's Stanley village to the right for two fields and then two overgrown enclosures to a double stile. Select the one on the left and follow the path a short distance to a lane.

Climb the stile opposite into a field, making a line to the wooden pole by the far hedge. Continue along the line of the poles to the opposite boundary, turning left for 75 yards to a stile. Cross and travel along the

Standish Wood and the panoramic dial.

back of some houses to exit via a metal squeezer stile, typical of the Stroud valley area, into Middleyard.

Turn left in front of the Baptist church along the road, shortly turning right along a lane beside Rosebank cattery. Look for a rough track on the right, which soon becomes a narrow path leading up a field to a lane. Turn left to continue to climb quite steeply up Pen Hill, eventually turning right into Stanley Wood.

The path levels out, hugging the side of the hill. Walk for about 1½ miles in a constant line, directly ahead, firstly through Stanley Wood and then Buckholt Wood, which are separated by an open field with an old house down the slope to the right. Emerge at the car park of Coaley Peak Country Park and picnic site.

The length of the Cotswold Way covered by this chapter is 12½ miles.

[10] Nympsfield
The Rose and Crown Inn

Nympsfield is a delightful village just a short distance from the escarpment edge. It has been highly commended several times in the annual Blediscoe Cup for the Best Kept Village and can get quite busy with visitors simply walking around its lanes enjoying the peace and tranquillity.

The Rose and Crown fits in perfectly with its surroundings and contributes positively to the community's efforts with its regular and impressive floral displays. Inside, a comfortable lounge bar, with a welcoming open fire in winter, and a dining area together house the many that come to enjoy this popular place. Outside, there is a very large garden containing a children's playground for use when the weather permits.

The inn has an excellent reputation for its interesting variations on the 'good pub food' theme. There are basket meals, sandwiches, ploughman's and a variety of hot dishes. It is open for food all day on Sunday and a succulent roast is served. There is also a children's menu. This is a freehouse offering Wadworth 6X, Marston's Pedigree, Boddingtons and ever-changing guest ales such as the local beers from the Wickwar and Uley breweries, which are well worth trying. Two draught lagers, draught stout and Newquay Steamer Bitter are also available.

The Rose and Crown lies just ½ mile from the Cotswold Way, 60 miles from the starting point in Chipping Campden. It offers good quality accommodation.
Telephone: 01453 860240.

How to get there: Nympsfield lies a short distance off the Stroud to Uley road, the B4066, about 6 miles from Stroud.

Parking: There is a car park opposite the pub for patrons and plenty of safe roadside parking in the village.

Length of the walk: Approximately 4 miles. OS maps: Pathfinders 1113 Stroud, 1112 Frampton on Severn and 1132 Dursley and Wotton-under-Edge, Landranger 162 Gloucester and Forest of Dean (inn GR 801004).

Starting from a delightful village, this is a mainly level walk, with just one fairly steep ascent. It runs along the escarpment edge past Nympsfield long barrow and Hetty Pegler's Tump (a detour of just ¼ mile) to the edge of Uley Bury, then returns through woodland.

The Walk
Walk away from the pub and village for ½ mile along the road signposted to Selsey and Stroud. At the meeting with the B4066 turn left and in 100 yards enter Coaley Peak Country Park and picnic site. As well as a spectacular viewing point there is the excavated Nympsfield long barrow to be studied.

Join the Cotswold Way as it traverses the car park from left to right to a kissing-gate on the far side of the park. Beyond is a panoramic dial from which the Way forks right along the escarpment edge onto a lower path through a small copse in an old quarry. Climb some steps to exit onto a road and turn left along the road for 75 yards past a milestone marker, to enter Coaley Wood.

Descend on the main path until it meets a metalled lane. Turn left and in a few yards bear left up the flight of steps. Follow the path to a gate and leave the Way here by passing through the gate, immediately turning right onto a bridleway leading to Uley Bury hill fort. Turn left along its edge, before bearing left down into the woods in 200 yards.

When the path meets a stile, do not cross it, but turn left downhill along a bridleway that can be muddy and slippery. At the road cross carefully to Crawley Lane, which is followed to its termination by a house. Turn right onto a footpath alongside the house and at the meeting of tracks continue straight ahead on a path which keeps close to the edge of Owlpen Wood.

At a fork bear right onto the lower path, which eventually ascends quite steeply out of the wood to emerge by a house. Continue to and cross a

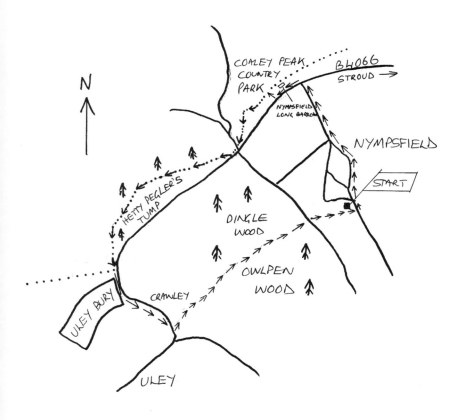

road, after which take the path hugging the wall and hedge on the left. As Nympsfield village is entered turn left to return to the start.

Cotswold Way – Coaley Peak to Cam Long Down

Walks 10 and 11 overlap for a few yards. Follow Walk 10 until the layby at a metal gate just before Uley Bury hill fort is reached. Join Walk 11, and leave Walk 10, by turning right down the gravel path descending directly away from the metal gate, which is followed to Cam Long Down.

The length of the Cotswold Way covered by this chapter 1½ miles.

[11] Uley
The Old Crown

Uley is a peaceful place, not one of the main tourist honeypots but nonetheless attractive. It is the home of a small independent brewery, found just off the main thoroughfare, which recently celebrated its tenth anniversary in its present incarnation, although brewing first took place in 1833. The village is said to have had 18 mills in the 18th century, producing the then famous Uley Blue cloth, though there is precious little evidence of their existence today. The church of St Giles is of Norman construction and commands a splendid position in the heart of the village.

The Old Crown Inn was once a farm cottage dating from 1638 but is now distinctively whitewashed externally, making it very photogenic. Opposite the church and behind a well-kept green, it is part of a picturesque scene. In addition to a beer garden at the rear there is also some seating to the front – a very pleasant spot to while away an hour or so. The interior comprises one large bar with separate areas for eating and drinking.

The pub attracts many regulars to enjoy the food and there is a good choice on offer from an imaginative set menu, served both at lunchtime and in the evening. As well as steak grills and fish dishes, vegetarian options are always available and everything is beautifully presented. A number of tables are set aside for diners but the pub can get quite busy so it is best to arrive in good time. As can be expected, the Old Crown is supplied by the local Uley Brewery and serves its Uley Bitter plus, on occasions, its other ales. This selection is supplemented by Whitbread WCPA, Boddingtons Bitter, draught lagers and stouts. For those who prefer a glass of wine with their meal a reasonable selection is also available.

The Old Crown Inn also offers accommodation and is situated about 1 mile off the Cotswold Way, approximately 64 miles from the start.

Telephone: 01453 860502.

How to get there: The Old Crown lies at the northern end of the village, on the B4066 Dursley to Selsey road.

Parking: The pub has a car park to the rear of the building and alternative parking can be found, if chosen carefully, on the roads nearby.

Length of the walk: Approximately 4½ miles. OS maps: Pathfinder 1132 Dursley and Wotton-under-Edge, Landranger 162 Gloucester and Forest of Dean (inn GR 792986).

This is a challenging walk involving three fairly sharp ascents, but the effort is rewarded with splendid views from Cam Long Down and a visit of great historical interest to Uley Bury hill fort.

The Walk
Cross the road towards the church, taking the footpath alongside the churchyard wall, which is signposted to Uley Bury. By an entrance to a house fork right to a kissing-gate. Gain the hill, aiming slightly left of a tree, detached from the wood, straight up the slope. A few yards beyond enter the wood in the top corner of the field and follow the path upwards, steering left of a wire fence to a stile.

Continue ahead to emerge on top of the hill at Uley Bury hill fort. The walk can be extended by going round the perimeter of the ancient fort, which takes about 20 minutes. To do this turn left when you reach the ramparts and walk three sides. The sheer size of the site is quite surprising and the detour is well worth while.

Those who do not tackle the circuit should turn right to walk one side of the fort, joining those who do at the north-west corner. Continue on the narrow path beside a wire fence to emerge at a layby.

Join the Cotswold Way by turning left down the gravel path, which leads to a farm. Round a small lake, turning right along a lane to enter a field via a stile by a barn. Walk straight up the slope towards the distinctive Cam Long Down.

At the base of the hill climb a flight of steps to enter a copse via a stile.

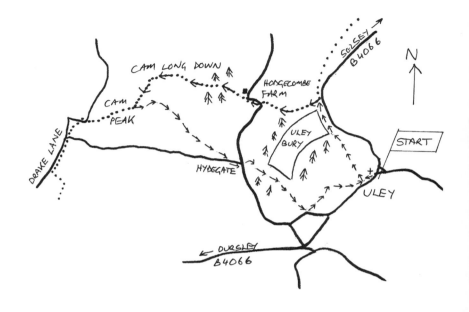

Turn left and continue to climb the steps, which lead onto Cam Long Down itself. As the ridge is traversed one of the best all-round views featured on the Cotswold Way can be had. In ¼ mile the path descends to a meeting of several tracks. Leave the Way by turning left onto the first track, into the undergrowth.

Walk through the ferns and pass through a wooden gate continuing ahead until you meet a rough lane. Turn right for 150 yards, taking the bridleway on the left, which ascends gently to a farm building. Continue on the lane to a junction and then on the bridleway opposite, marked 'Hyde Hill'.

Bear right in 75 yards to ascend to open ground, where the second track on the right should be taken into the trees. Follow the path to the left to a junction with another track in 30 yards. Turn right downhill, descending steeply and ignoring the marked footpath on the left, to a stile at the top of a field. Walk down to and then along the back of some houses to a stile by a field gate.

Continue past the detached house to another stile, cross a small section of a field to a kissing-gate and then take the path ahead, which leads past the church to emerge opposite the pub.

Cotswold Way – Cam Long Down to Dursley (1½ miles)

Leave Walk 11 in the dip between Cam Long Down and Cam Peak. Where Walk 11 turns left at the meeting of tracks, climb up to and then directly over Cam Peak, descending over a driveway to a house to a wooden gate. Turn left along the lane and then left again at a stile opposite Downhouse Farm.

Cross two fields to continue along a lane signposted to Dursley. About 100 yards after the entrance to Cam House school turn left and at the second stile turn right to walk across three fields to an iron kissing-gate by a farmhouse. Descend a flight of steps through a copse to emerge on the outskirts of Dursley.

Bear left up Long Street, walk to the right of the arcaded town hall building and continue along the pedestrian precinct. At the traffic lights turn left into May Lane to join Walk 12 at the Old Spot Inn.

The length of the Cotswold Way covered by this chapter is 3 miles.

[12]   **Dursley**
The Old Spot Inn

Dursley was once one of the main textile production centres in the area with all the natural ingredients available locally to make a successful industry. Today, it gives the feel of a community struggling to be self sufficient and is a mixture of 18th-century houses and modern day precincts. However, as the small town strives to make a living you are assured of a welcome and attention not always evident in the more illustrious centres along the Cotswold Way. Dursley has all the amenities that a weary walker might need after several days on the open footpaths and the ornate town hall and the 15th-century church provide the centrepiece from which to explore.

The Old Spot Inn is named after a breed of pig and the building dates from 1776. Not surprisingly, considering its name, there are plenty of photographs and mementoes (of pigs) around the interior of what is, essentially, one long bar. This is very much a locals' local, typified by the number of stools placed around the bar, but the atmosphere is delightfully welcoming to the visitor. There are two fireplaces, one at each end of the bar, and a chiming clock to signify the passing of time.

Although not purporting to be a food-orientated pub, the Old Spot still provides good things to eat. It particularly favours Cajun cooking, a spicy style from the southern states of America, and sandwiches are generally available. There are tables away from the main drinking area for dining but it should be noted that children under 14 are not permitted inside the pub. As for drinks, the superb Uley Old Spot, from the local brewery just down the road, is served plus Old Ric from the same source. A guest ale such as Gale's HSB is regularly on offer and the selection is complemented by draught Worthington and Bass. There is a beer garden to enjoy in the summer months.

The Old Spot Inn lies directly on the Cotswold Way, approximately 66 miles from Chipping Campden. It does not offer accommodation but this can be found elsewhere in the town – for example also on the Way itself is Mrs Daley's B&B at Highlands, Stinchcombe Hill (01453 542539).

Pub telephone: 01453 542870.

How to get there: Dursley lies on the A4135, a few miles from the M5 (best approached from junction 13). When the town centre is reached turn towards the bus station and the pub lies just around the corner.

Parking: The pub has no car park of its own but there is a free public one directly opposite.

Length of the walk: Approximately 4 miles. OS maps: Pathfinder 1132 Dursley and Wotton-under-Edge, Landranger 162 Gloucester and Forest of Dean (inn GR 754981).

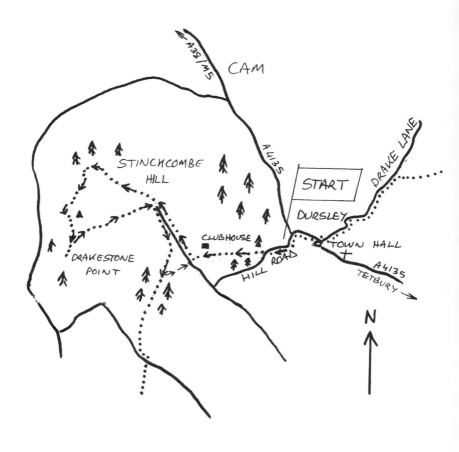

A brisk climb to Stinchcombe Hill and then a walk around the golf course, with some excellent views. This is an elevated route and marvellously bracing in the winter months.

The Walk

Immediately join the Cotswold Way by walking up Hill Road away from the pub to where the road bends to the left. Continue straight ahead into Westfield Wood onto a wide path and in a few yards bear left to climb steeply through the woods to emerge by the Stinchcombe Hill golf course clubhouse. The way lies ahead for a short distance, turning right onto a metalled road leading to a car park. Beware of golfers teeing off to the right!

Just past the car park leave the road to join a path curving to the left towards a wood in the distance. The path crosses two fairways so care and attention is required in both directions. Pass to the left of the wood and as the path begins to descend into the trees turn left by the 12th tee onto a perpendicular path. This leads to and turns left behind another tee, onto a rough track. The Sir Stanley Tubbs memorial shelter is soon reached with its glorious view of the Severn Vale. Continue along the edge of the escarpment, passing a panoramic dial and OS column to another memorial to Tubbs, this time a bench.

There is another excellent viewpoint just through the trees, but to continue the walk turn about to take the right path, which winds along the edge of the hill. Go below the car park passed before to the edge of Park Wood. Enter the trees briefly to avoid the golf course, then re-emerge for a short way to where the Way is waymarked for the second time into the wood.

Leave the Way at this point by turning 90° to the left to walk directly away from the wood. There is a clearly marked footpath across the golf course to the clubhouse. Retrace the path back down through Westfield Wood and Hill Road to return to the pub.

Cotswold Way – Stinchcombe Hill to Nibley Knoll (2 miles)

Leave Walk 12 when it turns left to return to the golf clubhouse by turning right into Park Wood. The path descends and widens, soon following the edge of the wood. Look for a footpath on the left, which at first descends but then quickly ascends via a flight of steps to a stile. Cross over a field, walking alongside the wire fence to a stile beneath an oak tree.

Continue down the slope of the adjacent field to a lane, turn left past the entrance to Park Farm House and immediately turn right onto a footpath signposted to North Nibley. Walk down the middle of a large field and a second smaller one to cross two stiles either side of a little enclosure. Turn right along the lane, passing the picturesque Mill House, to meet the B4060.

Go forward on the bridleway opposite to gently ascend to the village of North Nibley. Turn left along The Street, where there is bed and breakfast accommodation available (Nibley Cottage 01453 542794), to re-meet the B4060 opposite the Black Horse Inn, which also offers accommodation (01453 546841).

Walk along the B4060 for 100 yards to where there is a telephone box. Take the path over the road signposted to the Tyndale Monument, dedicated to William Tyndale who translated the Bible into English. Ignore the flight of steps on the right, although they do offer a short cut, and continue along the wooded hollow to where there is a signpost to the monument. The path takes a hairpin bend to a stile, which gives access to the hilltop that is known as Nibley Knoll and the monument itself.

The length of the Cotswold Way covered by this chapter is 4½ miles.

[13] Wotton-under-Edge
The Royal Oak Inn

Like many of its neighbours, Wotton once thrived on the cloth industry but this declined in the 19th century when the mill owners started to invest in land and buildings rather than local trade. Much of its architecture dates from this period although evidence of the town constructed in the 14th century, after the original was burnt down by King John's mercenaries, can be seen. Indeed the Ram Inn, which is now a private house and is said to be haunted, was built around 1350 – it lies just a few yards from the Cotswold Way on the minor road to Wortley. Today's town nestles below the slopes of the southern edge of the escarpment in a slightly elevated position, giving it a good view of the Vale of Berkeley. The main amenities lie along the principal street, which provides the spine of the present day community.

The Royal Oak Inn lies at one end of this spine and has two bars. The larger, the lounge bar, has a good sized dining area attached to it at the rear. The pub has an unpretentious feel and the decorations are subtle and understated, though there is plenty to interest the inquisitive visitor. The lounge bar has a small fireplace, giving added character. A few seats are available outside for warmer days.

The menu invites the visitor to sample good pub grub of the classic variety, including pan-fried trout, scampi, chicken Kiev and vegetable lasagne. There is also a range of grilled steaks. If a lighter meal is required the choice can be made from a variety of bar snacks, among them omelettes, basket meals and sandwiches. As the pub is a Whitbread tied house it is supplied with Flowers Original and Boddingtons Bitter plus draught Guinness and Murphy's stout. Blackthorn cider and draught lagers are also served.

The Royal Oak Inn offers bed and breakfast accommodation and lies a few yards from the Cotswold Way, just over 73 miles from the start at Chipping Campden.

Telephone: 01453 842316.

How to get there: Wotton lies south-west of Stroud, at the point where the B4058 and the B4060 meet. It can also be reached from junction 14 of the M5. The pub is in the centre of the town on Bear Street, close to its junction with the High Street.

Parking: The pub has a large car park of its own for patrons only. Alternative parking, if chosen carefully, can be found in the streets nearby.

Length of the walk: Approximately 4 miles. OS maps: Pathfinder 1132 Dursley and Wotton-under-Edge, Landranger 162 Gloucester and Forest of Dean (inn GR 755933).

The walk begins with a gradual climb up Wotton Hill and then becomes level and gentle through mainly woodland. There are good views from the Tyndale Monument and Jubilee Plantation.

The Walk

Starting with one's back to the pub, walk to the left, along the road to the junction. Cross to Tabernacle Pitch opposite, climbing to a footpath signposted to Coombe Hill alongside the former church, which now acts as auction rooms. Walk through a housing estate and gently climb the field beyond to a metalled lane.

Turning left along the lane to a T-junction, go left again and then almost immediately right onto a bridleway. This is followed, with a wood on the right and ignoring all paths leading into it, to a meeting of tracks. Take the second track on the left to a junction in 300 yards, turn left and, in a further 50 yards, right onto a footpath passing young trees to the right. The path gently descends into a wood to a major junction.

Turn right onto a bridleway which doubles as the Cotswold Way. Choose the higher path on the left to pass a broken gate in a copse and, on emerging into the open, follow the fence on the left across Nibley Knoll to the Tyndale Monument.

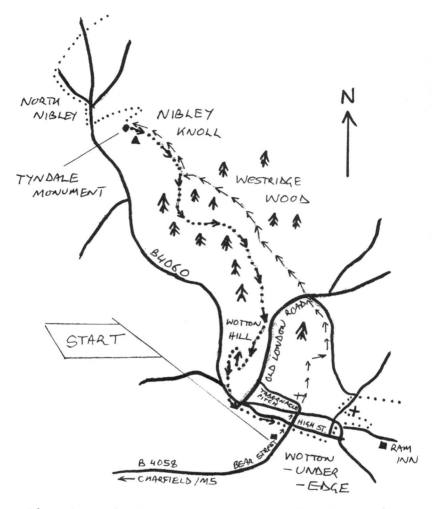

After enjoying the view, retrace the path back to Westridge Wood and at the major junction look for the Cotswold Way (bridleway) waymarkers on the trees. The first manoeuvre is the trickiest, a right and left from the crosstracks. Thereafter, carefully follow the markers until departing the path, but continuing on the Way, into a field on the right when the wood ends.

Stay beside field edge to a stile, descend Wotton Hill to, firstly, the Jubilee Plantation and then beyond as the path winds down the hill to the road. Turn left to walk into Wotton-under-Edge, arriving back at the pub via Bradley Street and Bear Street.

Cotswold Way – Wotton-under-Edge to Wortley (3 miles)

The Cotswold Way goes through the middle of Wotton-under-Edge via the High Street and Long Street, then bears left into Church Street. Cross to the raised walkway opposite and shortly fork right into Shinbone Alley, which winds itself through the houses into Church Walk as it crosses the churchyard. Turn right along the road to take the second lane on the right, which is called Valley Road.

In a few yards bear left and at the end of the lane proceed on a concrete footpath beside a brook. The path continues on the same line after crossing a lane to another, gained via a second squeezer stile. Gently ascend the lane in front of the houses to one called The Hive, where the Way turns left. Climb more steeply on the bridleway to a lane.

Turn left to walk across Blackquarries Hill, passing through a small copse, after which the Cotswold Way doubles back onto a gravel bridleway signposted to Tor Hill and Wortley. Leave the bridleway in 400 yards to pass through a field gate ahead. Follow a stone wall on the left to where it ends and the hill starts to drop away, at which point the path hugs the curved edge to enter a wood.

Immediately steer left up a flight of steps, emerging from the wood to turn right along a field track. Where this track swings left re-enter the wood ahead to descend steadily through a hollow to another farm track. Turn left to a stile before a lane. The Cotswold Way continues into the field opposite and is described in Walk 14.

The length of the Cotswold Way covered by this chapter is 5½ miles.

[14]   Hillesley
The Fleece Inn

Hillesley is a small village just a stone's throw from the pretty Kilcott valley. The memorial provides the focal point for the older part and is near to the start of the walk. There has been some development at the eastern end in recent times but this does not detract from the village's charm. It is surrounded by good walking country in all directions though this is often missed by those speeding along on the A46, which is to the east.

Just off the main road through the village, the white façade of the Fleece Inn catches the eye of those approaching from Wotton-under-Edge. The pub has two separate bars with an additional area set aside for dining. This is to be found off the lounge bar and provides a quiet spot in which to enjoy a meal, away from the bustle of the main drinking area, if this is preferred. The lounge bar has a fireplace and the interesting feature of a display of ceramic and pewter beer mugs hanging from the beam across the ceiling. In the summer months one can sit outside in either the spacious beer garden with its children's play area or there is a limited amount of seating at the front of the pub, adjoining Chapel Lane, from where the activity of the village can be observed.

There is a good choice of typical bar meals, including steak grills, fish dishes and lasagne. Lighter snacks such as omelettes, sandwiches and salads are also available. The evening menu is supplemented by blackboard specials and additional set meals, for example steak au poivre. Vegetarians will usually find an acceptable option. The inn is a Whitbread tied house and consequently offers Boddingtons Bitter, which originated from Manchester, and Flowers Original, which is a more traditional West Country real ale. The keg-delivered Poachers Bitter is served too. The stout drinker has two draught choices in Guinness and Murphy's, and there is draught Bulmers cider. Glasses of wine can be ordered to supplement a meal.

The Fleece Inn, which lies about 1 mile from the Cotswold Way at a point just over 77 miles from Chipping Campden, can provide accommodation.

Telephone: 01453 843189.

How to get there: Hillesley lies between Wotton-under-Edge and the A46, on a minor road. Just south of the memorial in Hillesley turn into Chapel Lane, which is on the bend, and the pub car park is a few yards further on.

Parking: There is a good sized car park belonging to the pub to the rear off Chapel Lane but very few alternative locations in the village as the lanes are quite narrow.

Length of the walk: Approximately 6 miles. OS maps: Pathfinders 1132 Dursley and Wotton-under-Edge and 1151 Patchway and Chipping Sodbury, Landranger 172 Bristol and Bath (inn GR 769896).

This is a pleasant, easy going, fairly level walk through several villages and hamlets along the Kilcott valley. A short detour towards the end of the circuit to the Somerset Monument is rewarding and offers a good view of the Vale of Berkeley.

The Walk

Take the road away from the pub that passes to the right of the memorial, beyond which there is a double bend. After the second bend cross the stile on the left at Longcroft Farm, traversing the field diagonally to a farm track. Bear 45° to the right across three fields, aiming for the bottom right corner.

Climb two stiles either side of a footbridge and then turn right to cross two further stiles separated by another footbridge. Follow the left field boundary for 75 yards to a stile, beyond which lies a young orchard. At the other side bear slightly right, with Park Farm on the left, to a stile beneath a beech tree.

Make a course to walk between the house and pond, turn right and then

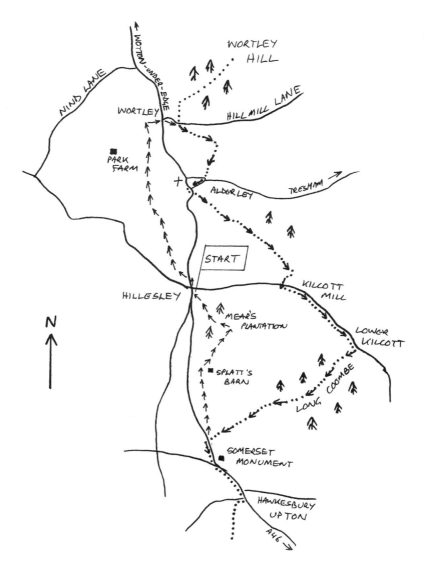

immediately left through a metal field gate. Proceed up the slope, ignoring the stile on the left, to a gate. Aim 100 yards to the left of the tennis court to join a track along the top boundary. Turn right along this track, which passes in front of a house, to the road passing through Wortley. Take the lane opposite beside Wortley Farm House, signposted to Ozleworth.

⌂ Soon after a double bend join the Cotswold Way by crossing the stile on the right into a field. The path is signposted to Alderley and Tresham. Cross, diagonally, the large field and then two smaller fields to join a bridleway. Follow this to the right and do not go over the stile ahead into a field. The bridleway follows a tree covered hollow to the village of Alderley. Cross the road and continue on the lane opposite to a junction with a road. Turn left beside a large house down a lane to a gate and join a bridleway, which is followed for ¾ mile to a junction with a rough track.

Some 200 yards to the right the track meets a lane. Turn left to walk past Kilcott Mill to the hamlet of Lower Kilcott, which is approximately ½ mile away. Look for a bridleway to the right, which gently ascends through the woods to a field gate. Turn right immediately into a large enclosure, exiting from the top left corner via the first stile on the left into Frith Wood. In a short while emerge into a field, turning right to aim for a farm building beside a road, at which the Cotswold Way continues left to the Somerset Monument, which commemorates General Lord Somerset who served at Waterloo.

Leave the Way here by returning along the road to where it bends left and continue straight ahead onto a bridleway. When the farm buildings are reached turn right onto a footpath. Soon cross a stile and then follow the field edge to just beyond a wood. Turn left to enter Mear's Plantation through a field gate. Descend through the wood and across two fields to emerge in the lane by the pub.

⌂ **Cotswold Way – Somerset Monument to Horton (2½ miles)**
Proceed along the road from the monument to Hawkesbury Upton. At the start of the village turn right by a small pond onto a metalled lane. In 100 yards bear left onto a bridleway signposted to Horton, which is followed for 1 mile to a metal gate. Do not gain the lane but switch to the adjacent field and walk parallel to it for two fields.

At the third field aim down the slope to the right of the barn but do not enter the next field. Instead turn right to walk along its outside edge onto some rough ground and then into a wood. Where the path descends into a hollow turn right, going out of the trees and across some pasture to a lane by Horton Court. Turn left along the lane to Horton village, where it meets and joins Walk 15.

The length of the Cotswold Way covered by this chapter is 6½ miles.

[15]   Old Sodbury
The Dog Inn

Old Sodbury, like its neighbour Little Sodbury, lies on the Cotswold Way as it descends from the escarpment. There has been a settlement here for centuries, as the Iron Age hill fort testifies. The origin of 'sod' is undetermined, though 'bury' is accepted as meaning a fort or camp. Old Sodbury is so named as it is the original settlement of the three villages in close proximity bearing the 'Sodbury' name.

The Dog Inn lies on the busy A432 and whilst the exterior is colourful and attractive it belies the traditional character to be found inside. There is one large bar, which is oak beamed and has a large, inviting fireplace at one end, and plenty of tables and places to sit. A beer garden will be found outside, with a children's play area to the rear.

One of the most extensive menus in the area is offered here – for example, grilled steaks, chicken dishes, curries, fish and an amazing 18 vegetarian choices. If a menu cannot be located most meals are displayed in a novel manner on cards around the bar area. There are also blackboard specials, sandwiches and a children's list. The drinker is equally spoilt for choice as the pub serves the excellent Wickwar Bob, from the local brewery, Flowers Original and Wadworth 6X. There are also two draught ciders and lagers. For those cold winter walks there is a first class selection of classic malt whiskies to warm frozen feet! As to be expected in a pub where good food is a priority wine by the glass is served, plus speciality coffees to complete the culinary experience.

The Dog Inn offers accommodation and lies directly on the Cotswold Way, 85 miles from Chipping Campden.

Telephone: 01454 312006.

How to get there: Old Sodbury lies on the A432, between its junction with the A46 and Chipping Sodbury. The pub is at the bottom of a hill, about 1½ miles from the A46.

Parking: There is a car park to the side of the pub and some roadside parking away from the main road.

Length of the walk: Approximately 5 miles. OS maps: Pathfinder 1151 Patchway and Chipping Sodbury, Landranger 172 Bristol and Bath (inn GR 754815).

There is a sharp ascent to the escarpment followed by a hilltop walk before you descend to visit two historic villages and an ancient hill fort.

The Walk

Walk away from the pub uphill along the left pavement of the A432, turning left into Church Lane. At The Gatehouse turn right up a flight of steps onto a footpath signposted to Little Sodbury and Badminton. Cross a stile to climb steeply, diagonally over a field to a copse and on emerging follow the right field edge to meet the A46.

Do not leave the field but turn half-left back across the field, aiming for a line of trees. Pass through a gap in the stone wall separating two fields to continue on the same line. Enter the hill fort area over a stile and walk to the right around the mounds, which will give you some indication of its immense size, to some farm buildings.

Leave the enclosure via a stile which carries the familiar Cotswold Way marker, and where the path is indicated left and downwards, turn right through a field gate and then immediately left through another into a field. The footpath actually lies across the field but it is indistinct and therefore you will find it easier to follow the left boundary until a stile is met. Walk along New Tyning Lane opposite, which is signposted to Horton, turning left to the village itself.

⌂ In Horton the Cotswold Way joins from the right along the lane from Hawkesbury and Horton Court but continue beyond this junction for a few yards to turn left onto a footpath signposted to Little Sodbury.

Steer left past the entrance to a house, crossing a stile to walk to the right

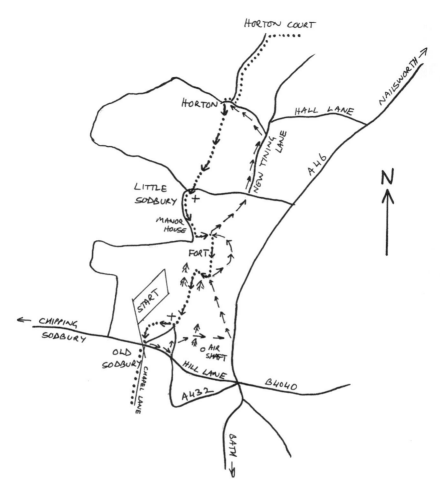

of a field divider and, where this swings left, continue ahead to the opposite boundary. Walk across four fields to a farmhouse, turning right along the lane. At the junction turn left towards Old Sodbury, passing Little Sodbury church. The road leads out of the village and in ¼ mile the Cotswold Way is indicated left onto a driveway to a house.

Immediately, though, turn right onto a track which climbs up through the wood to the farmhouse visited earlier on the walk. Re-enter the hill fort area but this time walk directly over the middle to a familiar stile. Turn right here to descend through Little Sodbury Wood to where the path becomes grassy and then turn sharp left. Cross a stile to follow the lower

Little Sodbury church.

field boundary to the back of a farmyard.

Go over a stile beyond onto a path that emerges by Old Sodbury school. Enter the churchyard opposite and then exit via an iron kissing-gate, where there are good views of the Severn Vale. Descend the field slightly to the left to a stile, which is crossed, and then the path lies across the field to a farmyard. Walk through this yard to Cotswold Lane, which leads back to the pub.

Cotswold Way – Old Sodbury to Dodington Park (¾ miles)

Walk along Chapel Lane, which lies beside the pub, for ¼ mile, looking for a stile on the left clearly marked as the Cotswold Way. Walk over four fields to gain an elevated position, eventually meeting a lane at Coomb's End. Turn right along the road to just after the junction with Chapel Lane, signposted to Chipping Sodbury, where the Way enters the outskirts of Dodington Park by taking a path signposted on the left to Tormarton and joins Walk 16.

The length of the Cotswold Way covered by this chapter is 3 miles.

[16] Tormarton
The Portcullis Inn

Tormarton is a peaceful village, free from traffic though not from its noise as the M4 passes just a short distance away and there is a constant hum in the air. However, do not let this detract from your visit as those whizzing by will miss the splendid St Mary Magdalene church and a fine Cotswold pub.

The stone-built, ivy-clad Portcullis Inn lies in the centre of the village, near to the church. It has a large, L-shaped bar, an additional section set aside solely for diners and, outside to the rear, a beer garden. There is a friendly atmosphere and you will find plenty of local people with whom to discuss the area.

The food menu is displayed on a large blackboard that dominates one end of the bar. An extensive choice is offered, including jacket potatoes, salads, vegetarian meals, curries and fish dishes. For those with heartier appetites, there are steak grills and a very tempting and imaginative sweet selection to follow. A children's menu is also available. This is a freehouse serving a good range of real ales, among them Courage Best, Wadworth 6X, Butcombe Bitter from the brewery formed in Bristol in 1978, the more travelled Otter Ale from the Otter Brewery in Honiton, Devon, and John Smith's Bitter. Draught Guinness and two draught lagers – Stella

Artois and Carlsberg – complete the selection.

The pub, which offers accommodation, lies directly on the Cotswold Way, 88 miles from Chipping Campden but more significantly only 16 miles from Bath.

Telephone: 01454 218263.

How to get there: Tormarton is only ½ mile from the A46 at a point just north of junction 18 of the M4.

Parking: The pub has a good sized car park and alternative parking can be found in the quiet roads around the village.

Length of the walk: Approximately 4 miles. OS maps: Pathfinder 1167 Bristol (East), Landranger 172 Bristol and Bath (inn GR 768787).

An easy-going stroll along country lanes and in the parkland of Dodington Park. Although the A46 is crossed twice and the M4 is nearby, this walk is pleasantly free of most traffic.

The Walk

Walk along the gravel driveway beside the pub to a stile, cross the field and in the next follow the stone wall to the left along two sides to the opposite corner. Turn right along the lane for ¼ mile to the junction with the A46.

Cross to the B4465 opposite and just around the corner turn right along the lane signposted to Dodington. This is a little-used road but it is narrow in places so care and attention should be paid while you follow it for 1 mile to the hamlet of Dodington.

A further ¼ mile on you will meet the Cotswold Way again as it approaches in the opposite direction by some houses. Turn right onto a footpath signposted to Tormarton, into Dodington Park. Walk straight ahead, crossing two stiles either side of a lane, to a gate by a footbridge. Bear left to the top of the slope and at the next stile by a field gate steer left of a solitary tree and then around the edge of a wood. Cross a stile into the next field and proceed, with the wire fence on the left, to the opposite corner and another stile.

The clearly defined path goes straight ahead to a footbridge and stile that straddles a brook. Aim left up the bank to a stile and in a few yards emerge on the busy and fast A46. Cross very carefully to a stile by an unusual mile marker opposite.

Walk over two fields separated by a road to a lane, climb some stone steps and then aim diagonally across to the opposite corner of the next field. Turn left along the road for a few yards before entering a field on the

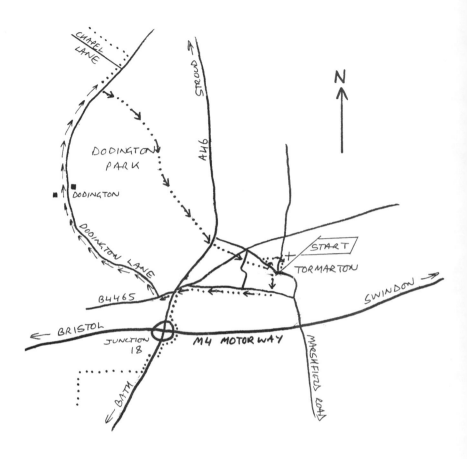

right. Walk to the line of trees on the far side, turn right past the church and right again at the junction to return to the pub.

⌂ Cotswold Way – Tormarton (A46) to Dyrham Park (3 miles)
Leave Walk 16 where it crosses the A46 for the first time by turning left along the main road towards Bath. Cross the motorway to the left of the roundabout and then where there is a gap in the central reservation switch to the other side of the A46. Walk along the grass verge for 150 yards to turn right into a public amenity area.

The Cotswold Way continues through the car park into the field beyond, through some trees. Turn left to follow the field edge, ignoring

An ancient wayside sign, seen on the route.

the first unmarked path, to a waymarked bridleway into the adjacent field. Walk with a hedge on the right across two large fields under the power lines to a road. Continue along Field Lane opposite to meet some farm buildings, where the Way turns right, signposted to Dyrham, to follow a stone wall and join Walk 17.

The length of the Cotswold Way covered by this chapter is 5½ miles.

[17] Pennsylvania
The Swan Inn

Pennsylvania claims to have connections with the famous William Penn, who gave his name to the more notable location in the United States of America. Whether or not there is any basis in fact for this proclamation it is fascinating to hear a local tell the story. The community itself is little more than a hamlet on the very busy A46 but few would deny it its claim to fame.

It is difficult to believe that a more friendly reception along the Cotswold Way can be had than in the Swan Inn, which is a family run affair with those serving the beer and food having a familiar look about them. This is a fairly small pub with an unpretentious character and the accommodation is spread around the single bar. There is a separate dining area for families, which is 'no smoking', and an outside garden for warmer days. The pub is particularly welcoming to walkers.

The food typifies the whole atmosphere of the pub as it also is comforting and hearty. Ploughman's lunches and sandwiches are almost always available, whilst hot dishes such as chilli con carne, braised steak, jacket potatoes and more than one vegetarian meal regularly feature. On Sunday lunchtimes a roast dinner with all the trimmings is served. As for drinks, two excellent ales from the Otter Brewery in Devon immediately catch the eye but spare a thought also for George's Bitter from Bristol, Morland Old Speckled Hen, Marston's Pedigree or John Smith's Bitter. Stout lovers will be tempted by the draught Beamish and there are two draught lagers and a cider. The Swan Inn does not offer accommodation, however Cold Ashton is only a mile or so away – try Mrs Williamson's B&B at High Lanes (01225 891255). The Swan is 93½ miles from Chipping Campden and 10½ miles from Bath.

Pub telephone: 01225 891022.

How to get there: The pub is situated on the A46 just ½ mile from its junction with the A420, midway between junction 18 of the M4 and the city of Bath.

Parking: The pub has its own car park but due to its location on the A46 there are few safe alternative locations.

Length of the walk: Approximately 5½ miles, with a shorter option, cutting out Hinton Hill, of approximately 4 miles. OS maps: Pathfinder 1167 Bristol (East), Landranger 172 Bristol and Bath (inn GR 744734).

A fairly easy walk across farmland, with a good viewing point from Hinton Hill and a visit to the very peaceful village of Dyrham.

The Walk

Walk away from the pub to the petrol station, turning back along a lane signposted to Dyrham. In 75 yards turn left onto a footpath that leads across a field. Before reaching the gate turn right to pass in front of a line of pine trees to a road. Cross the stile opposite into the field, aiming towards a line of trees, but 50 yards before reaching them turn right to walk parallel to the line to a stile.

Descend diagonally to the right, cross a stile and choose the path to the right, which leads to another field. Bear left across this field to a gate, pass through and immediately double back into the adjacent field. Turn left immediately to follow the hedge to a stile.

Cross another stile on the right and on emerging in a field follow the right boundary to exit through the first gap in the hedge. Cross two fields to Lower Ledge Farm, pass to the left of a small pond and leave by a stile at the far end. Over the yard is a further stile. Turn left and make a trail for the tall tree on the far side.

Use the stile under the tree to follow the field edge to a lane. Turn right to Dyrham, where the walk can be shortened by turning right at the junction to go through the centre of the village. Walk 17 and the Cotswold Way are met at the far end by the bench on the small green and continue to the right back to Pennsylvania.

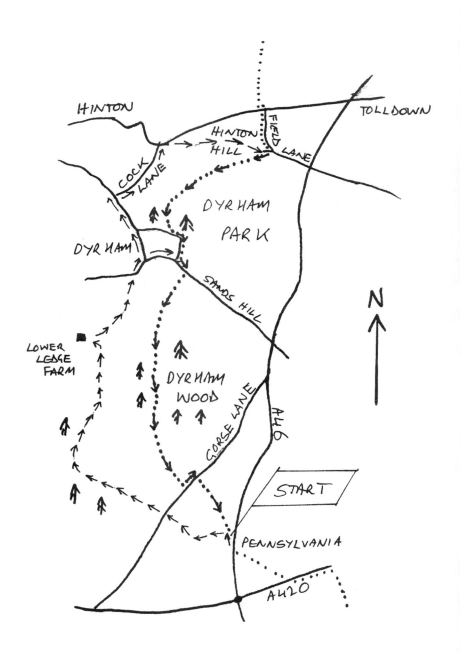

HINTON

TOLLDOWN

HINTON HILL

FIELD LANE

COCK LANE

DYRHAM PARK

DYRHAM

STANDS HILL

N

LOWER LEDGE FARM

DYRHAM WOOD

GORSE LANE

A46

START

PENNSYLVANIA

A420

82

To continue the main walk, do not enter Dyrham village but proceed along the road, signposted to Hinton, taking the second road on the right, which is called Cock Lane. At the next junction bear right and immediately cross a stile on the right giving access to Hinton Hill.

Walk across the top of the ancient hill fort, with the good views that make this extended walk even more worth while, then descend on the far side into the corner of a field. Cross to the next field and then take the path up the bank to the far corner where the Cotswold Way is joined by the stone wall boundary of Dyrham Park.

Turn right to follow the stone wall until it enters a wood. Walk through then turn left along the lane that leads past the manor house into Dyrhan village. At the bench on the little green join the shorter version of the walk by turning left. In a short way take a path to the right, then follow the Cotswold Way markers across several fields.

After crossing a footbridge over a brook steer left up the slope to the top left corner and enter Dyrham Wood, in which there is a message book for you to record your thoughts and experiences for those that follow! On emerging, pass to the right of a farm building and follow the stone wall to a road.

Turn left for 75 yards along Gorse Lane before entering a field on the right. The path follows the hedge on the right, back to the pub.

Cotswold Way – Pennsylvania to Cold Ashton (½ mile

Opposite the petrol station is a stile giving access to a field. This and the following field are crossed diagonally to meet the A420. Turn left and in a short way you will reach the White Hart, which is the start to Walk 18.

The length of the Cotswold Way covered by this chapter is 2½ miles.

[18] Cold Ashton
The White Hart

Cold Ashton is not to be confused with the village of a similar name in north Gloucestershire. In fact, so many people did get muddled that the Gloucestershire village changed its name to Aston Blank, though Cold Aston can still be seen on many fingerposts and signs. The Avon version is a quiet and peaceful place, set back from two major trunk roads and commanding a splendid valley view from the road in front of the Old Rectory and Manor House. After the battle of Lansdown Hill, a few miles to the south-west of the village, which took place during the Civil War, the Royalist troops brought their wounded, and their deceased leader Sir Bevil Grenville, to the Manor House. A monument to Sir Bevil is featured further along the Cotswold Way.

The White Hart is known to the locals as the 'Folly' and was originally a farm, becoming an inn during the early 17th century. It is detached from Cold Ashton, though not by far, and lies on the old coaching route from Bristol to London, which is now the A420. Inside, there is plenty of room to sit and admire the wood panelling, oak beams and the horsemanship memorabilia decorating the walls. There is a fireplace centrally located and, outside, a beer garden with a children's play area to the rear.

The food menu relies on tried and tested pub favourites to satisfy its customers, many of whom are 'passing trade'. There are grilled steaks, ploughman's lunches, salads and home-made pies. Vegetarians have at least two options, including the farmhouse escalope packed with fresh and varied vegetables. The usual bar snacks can also be ordered if a lighter meal is required, plus desserts and coffees for those who want to linger a while. The inn is an Ushers of Trowbridge tied house and serves its own Best Bitter. The brewery has become independent again since 1991 after three decades of control by the national breweries. Ushers ales are supplemented by Wadworth 6X, also from Wiltshire, and draught Guinness. Two draught lagers – Foster's and Carlsberg – are sold, together with a good range of bottled beers.

The White Hart does not offer accommodation, but this is available at Whittington farmhouse (01225 891628) which lies a short distance along the footpath, opposite the entrance to the pub's car park. The inn lies on the Cotswold Way, 94 miles from Chipping Campden and only 10 miles from the end of the walk in Bath.

Pub telephone: 01225 891233.

How to get there: The pub lies along the A420 Bristol to Chippenham road, just ½ mile east from its intersection with the A46.

Parking: There is a large car park which accommodates 100 cars, but this is locked outside opening times. However, there are some other spaces belonging to the pub, alongside the A420.

Length of the walk: Approximately 5 miles. OS maps: Pathfinder 1167 Bristol (East), Landranger 172 Bristol and Bath (inn GR 749730).

This is a rambling good walk amongst undulating hills, giving some fine valley views.

The Walk

Immediately join the Cotswold Way by crossing the road to a kissing-gate opposite the entrance to the car park. Follow the footpath alongside the stone wall to the churchyard, beyond which is Hyde's Lane. Turn right to walk past the Manor House, where there are excellent views of the valley, and then through Cold Ashton village. At the last house Hyde's Lane steers right but the Way departs here down the slope to the A46.

Opposite is Greenway lane, which is followed for ¾ mile until it descends sharply, just past some farm buildings, aiming for a lake that can be seen in the distance over the trees. Where the lane swings left enter the trees on the right, shortly emerging to cross two fields beyond, with the lake on the left, to some more farm buildings.

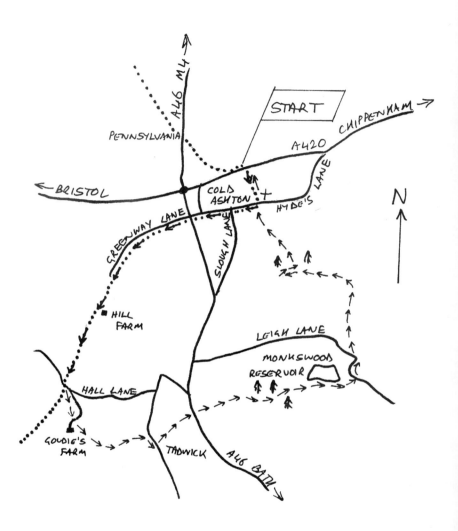

Turn left, but in 50 yards bear right over a cattle grid to a second a little further on. At this point leave the Cotswold Way, which goes up the slope to the right, by continuing along a metalled lane. Some 50 yards before it passes through a hedgerow bear 45° up the slope to a stile, over which the indistinct path crosses the lane to pass beneath Goudie's Farm. At the far end of the house cross a stile into the next field.

Aim down the field to a point two thirds along the bottom boundary and cross a metal footbridge. On the other side walk directly up the bank to leave this field via a stile in front of a farmhouse. Turn right along the lane through the hamlet of Tadwick to just beyond Tadwick Cottage, then climb the steps on the left to enter a field. Go up the slope around the back of the cottage to enter the next field via some more steps by a wooden pole. Greater effort is required to proceed upwards over two stiles to the A46.

Cross to a path opposite, which leads over the middle of a field to a gate, then pass through to follow the right field boundary to the right corner. Over the stile, descend the slope for 100 yards, looking for a further stile on the left, beyond which the path hugs the base of the hill to enter a wood.

Traverse the footbridge on the right and, a few yards on, turn left to walk beside Monkswood Reservoir. At the lane turn left to climb past the buildings, beyond which you leave the lane at a bend to join a footpath that leads down a slope. At a second stile and gate combination bear right around the base of the hillock to a third stile and gate. Cold Ashton can be seen up the hill to the right.

Continue straight ahead through two more gate/stiles and, where the track forks onto a higher and lower path, double back to take the almost hidden path into the woods. Turn left through a gate to aim directly up the valley, keeping the brook on the right until a waymarker beneath an oak tree points the path slightly to the left up the slope.

Climb an unusual three-tier wooden stile, beyond which you should aim for a gate to the right of the house. Turn right to retrace the path back through the churchyard to the pub.

Cotswold Way – Hall Lane to Hanging Hill (1½ miles)

Leave Walk 18 at the second cattle grid at the start of Hall Lane by steering right up the slope to cross three fields to meet a bridleway. Turn right and 150 yards beyond a metal gate climb the bank and stile over a stone wall into a field.

Keep to the right field edge until the path passes through a wood to emerge by the Grenville Monument. Continue to the road, cross and walk along the driveway leading to the Avon Fire Brigade Headquarters. Steer to the right at the entrance and almost immediately left to walk beside the wire perimeter fencing. Pass through a gate and continue alongside a stone wall and fence to an OS column marking the summit of Hanging Hill. Join Walk 19 at this point.

The length of the Cotswold Way covered by this chapter is 4 miles.

[19]   Upton Cheyney
The Upton Inn

Upton Cheyney is a delightful village, with very little through traffic to destroy its peaceful atmosphere. It enjoys an elevated position just away from the main escarpment and has good views across the Avon valley. There is very little modern development in the village and it retains its tranquillity as most visitors do not venture beyond the excellent pub, which lies at its south-western end.

The Upton Inn is a colourful building, clad as it is virtually all over in ivy. It has been extended in recent years to give additional accommodation but this is barely noticeable from the road. Inside, it is devoted to providing an enjoyable evening or lunchtime in comfortable surroundings and despite the remoteness of the village it is a very popular establishment. On entering, there is a reception/drinking area around a semi-circular bar but many people come again and again for the food. Most of the pub is laid out with tables for dining and there is also a separate restaurant area. Unusually, the walls are decorated with European and Eastern rugs.

The food menu is excellent. As it is ever changing, however, it is not possible to predict what will be on offer. Suffice to say that all meals are made with fresh, local, seasonal produce and are imaginatively prepared. Vegetarians should note that their choice may be a little limited though no less appetising. Although a food-orientated pub, the Upton Inn still offers some good ales to supplement the meals. It is a freehouse serving Wadworth 6X and other guest ales, also draught lager and stout. As is to be expected, the range of wines is more extensive. The whites can be seen chilling in the ice bucket on the bar and the reds warming to room temperature to the rear. There is also a good selection of bottled drinks of all varieties.

The inn, which does not offer accommodation, lies about a mile from the Cotswold Way, making it quite a detour, although a worthwile one, for those doing the long distance path. This walk joins the Way at the Hanging Hill OS column, which is 97½ miles from Chipping Campden and 6½ from Bath Abbey.

Telephone: 0117 9324489.

How to get there: Upton Cheyney is signposted north off the A431 Bath to Bristol road between the settlements of Swineford and Bitton.

Parking: The pub has its own good sized car park and alternative parking can be found, if careful and considerate, in the surrounding lanes.

Length of the walk: Approximately 6 miles. OS maps: Pathfinders 1183 Bath and Keynsham and 1167 Bristol (East), Landranger 172 Bristol and Bath (inn GR 692699).

This is a very rewarding walk. After passing through two small and pleasant Avon villages, it climbs steeply to the escarpment, then follows its edge, with great views of the Avon valley and Bath, before gently returning through pretty North Stoke.

The Walk

Walk up the lane from the pub as far as the old school house, where an elevated stile gives access to a field. Cross to the house opposite, turning right to follow the field boundary to a double stile. Continue beyond, across several fields, to join a farm track that becomes a metalled lane into the hamlet of Beach.

At the junction turn right to follow Beach Lane to another junction, with a footpath beside Hanging Hill Cottages opposite. Climb the steep, rough track, pass through a gate and continue up the path that bears to the right. Climb the slope at all times to the summit of Hanging Hill, which is marked by an OS column, and join the Cotswold Way at this point.

Walk in the same direction across the hill, with views to the right, alongside a stone wall to meet a golf course green. Cross the outside of this green to a track, turn left and follow the edge of a wood. At the end of the trees, turn right alongside another stone wall, pass through

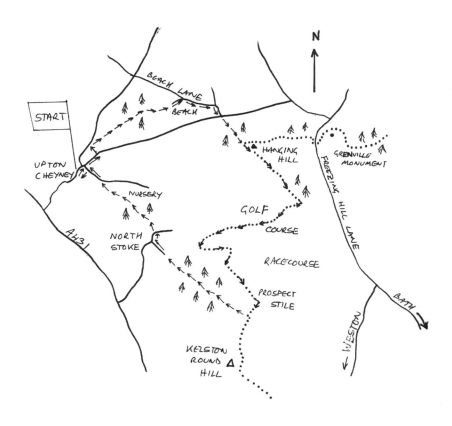

a metal gate and, where the path descends, bear left up to another gate.

After a further 400 yards the path swings left up to a gate and stile, beyond which the racecourse grandstand can be seen. At a gap in a stone wall turn right to walk around the outside edge of the course to Prospect Stile, where the first glimpse of Bath can be seen. Descend the left field boundary below to a hunting gate, where the walk departs the Cotswold Way by turning right along a bridleway.

This narrow path leads, in ¾ mile, to North Stoke. Bear right in the village and at Chestnut Barn turn left along a rough track. Cross a stile by a gate on the right into a field, taking the path that aims diagonally into the next field. Enter the wood partway down the slope by an ash tree, marked by a wooden post, cross a footbridge over a stream and, on emerging, bear left to aim for a stile below the greenhouses.

Over the stile, turn right to follow the field edge to a gate by a lane. Continue ahead to a junction, at which the pub lies down the lane to the left.

⌂ Cotswold Way – Prospect Stile to Sion Hill (3½ miles)

Leave Walk 19 at the hunting gate in the bottom corner of the field below Prospect Stile by going through it and immediately turning right through another, onto a bridleway. This is followed, as it steers to the left of Kelston Round Hill where it can get very muddy, to join a lane in ½ mile.

In a few yards cross the stile on the right to walk across the top of a field to the OS column at Penn Hill. The path starts to descend but soon diverts to the left through the trees, across some open ground and then a playing field to a gate in the right-hand corner. Turn left towards Weston, taking the second left, called Penn Hill Road.

Use the pedestrian crossing to turn right into High Street and almost immediately bear left into Church Street in front of the terraced houses. At the far end of the churchyard turn left up the lane, at the top of which the Way turns right through a housing estate. A footpath at the end of the first road off to the left, which is a 'no through road', winds around the back of the houses and then across a field.

Over a brook, the path climbs to Primrose Hill and then continues along a passage way giving access to Summerfield Road. In a short way turn right down Sion Hill, which bends to the left and then enters Approach Golf Course. Midway down the slope a concrete footpath attaches from the left and from here to the end of the Cotswold Way at Bath Abbey the directions in Walk 20 are to be followed.

The length of the Cotswold Way covered by this chapter is 5 miles.

[20]   Bath
The Huntsman

Bath is a wonderful place in which to finish the Cotswold Way as it is steeped in history and has any number of attractions for the visitor. It is very popular with tourists of all nationalities. The Way ends gloriously at the Abbey/Roman Baths but allow extra time to get to know this small city, with its splendid architecture and unique atmosphere. The walk starts from near the Abbey and takes in just a few of the local sights and points of interest but it is highly recommended that you undertake a little further exploration. You will not be disappointed.

The Huntsman lies right beside the Abbey and therefore offers either a welcome finale to those completing the long distance walk or a central point from which to explore the delights of Bath. Parts of the inn date from the 15th century and it is situated in one of the oldest parts of the city. Indeed, the hostelry has several claims to fame as to its past customers, including Jane Austen. Today it is as popular as ever, with a steady stream of visitors and townsfolk entering the narrow doorway, beyond which is a long bar and plenty of seating. It can be quite entertaining to watch the comings and goings which occur throughout the day, as this is a very busy pub. There is also a separate restaurant area and cellar bar.

Fortunately for the walker, the Hunstman is open for long hours and food is served nearly all the time, including late into the evening. This can be reassuring for those on the long distance path, whose expected time of arrival cannot always be predicted. The menu is quite extensive and includes steak and kidney pie, cottage pie, cauliflower au gratin, cannelloni, large sandwiches, jacket potatoes with a variety of fillings and salads. There are also numerous sweets. In short, the menu is packed with basic pub favourites, which the hungry rambler will welcome. The inn is an Eldridge Pope tied house, whose brewery is situated in Dorchester, Dorset. It serves some particularly fine West Country ales, including the very strong Royal Oak, Thomas Hardy Country Bitter, Best and Dorchester Bitter plus a guest beer. Draught stout and cider are also served. Also, as the inn provides a steady supply of meals there is a greater range of wines than to be found in many pubs.

The only thing the Hunstman does not provide is accommodation, but lying in the heart of Bath as it does there are many facilities of all standards available close by. The inn is at the end of the Cotswold Way – 104 miles from Chipping Campden. There is a very well organised central booking service (fee) for accommodation in and around Bath, which is available at the TIC in Abbey Churchyard, at the end of the Cotswold Way.

Pub telephone: 01225 460100.

How to get there: The Huntsman lies at the very heart of Bath, close to the Abbey. It is probably advisable to find a public car park in the centre and walk to the pub.

Parking: The pub itself has no car park and its location means that facilities near to it are few. However, Bath is a busy city designed to accommodate visitors and therefore there are many public parking areas not too far away.

Length of the walk: Approximately 2½ miles. OS maps: Pathfinder 1183 Bath and Keynsham, Landranger 172 Bristol and Bath (inn GR 753647).

This is essentially a short town walk but can be extended in any variety of ways and, unless time is short, it would be a shame not to take the opportunity to explore and enjoy this splendid city.

The Walk

Walk directly away from the pub, over the bridge, using the left pavement. At the far side of the bridge descend the stairway to the river Avon, turning right to walk close to the river past the rugby ground. Climb some more steps to cross back over the river, using Pulteney Bridge, gain the road past the shops and turn right into the High Street.

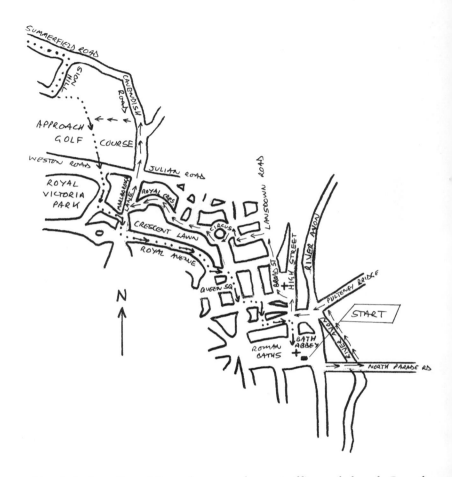

Bear left along Broad Street between the post office and church. Pass the Postal Museum and continue over the traffic lights into Lansdown Road. In a few yards the walk turns left into Alfred Street but should a visit to either the Building of Bath Museum or the British Folk Art Collection be on your agenda turn right at this point.

The Assembly Rooms and the Museum of Costume lie just around the corner, beyond which is also the Museum of East Asian Art. At this point turn left into the Circus, constructed between 1754 and 1769, noticing the acorns adorning the top of the buildings all the way around. The walk continues directly over into Royal Crescent, which was constructed slightly later, between 1767 and 1775, by the same architect, John Wood.

Bath Abbey – seen from the walk route.

At the far end of this splendid architectural achievement turn right into Marlborough Buildings to the junction with Julian Road by a pub. Continue over into Cavendish Road, signposted to the Bath College of Higher Education, and in 200 yards turn left across the Approach Golf Course on a concrete footpath. Where it meets some railings join the Cotswold Way by turning left.

Cross the road into the Royal Victoria Park, walking beside the railings as the pavement passes the memorial. Continue along Royal Avenue, with Royal Crescent to the left, and on leaving the park via Queens Parade turn left into Queen Square.

In the opposite corner go left into Wood Street, then Quiet Street before turning right into New Bond Street. The path now becomes a pedestrian only one as New Bond Street Place, then Union Passage and finally Abbey Churchyard, marking the end of Walk 20 and the Cotswold Way itself.

The length of the Cotswold Way covered by this chapter is 1 mile.

Tourist Information Centres

Chipping Campden – Woolstaplers Hall Museum, High Street, Glos GL55 6HB (tel: 01386 840101)

Broadway – 1 Cotswold Court, Worcs WR12 7AA (tel: 01386 852937)

Winchcombe – Town Hall, High Street, Glos GL54 5LJ (tel: 01242 602925)

Cheltenham – 77 Promenade, Glos GL50 1PP (tel: 01242 522878)

Painswick – The Library, Stroud Road, Glos GL6 6DT (tel: 01452 813552)

Stroud – Subscription Rooms, George Street, Glos GL5 1AE (tel: 01453 765768)

Bath – Abbey Chambers, Abbey Churchyard, Avon BA1 1LY (tel: 01225 462831)